LIFE IS A STARTUP

LIFE IS A STARTUP

WHAT FOUNDERS CAN TEACH US

ABOUT MAKING CHOICES

AND MANAGING CHANGE

NOAM WASSERMAN

STANFORD BUSINESS BOOKS
AN IMPRINT OF STANFORD UNIVERSITY PRESS
STANFORD, CALIFORNIA

Stanford University Press

Stanford, California

© 2019 by Noam Wasserman. All rights reserved.

Special discounts for bulk quantities of Stanford Business Books are available to corporations, professional associations, and other organizations. For details and discount information, contact the special sales department of Stanford University Press. Tel: (650) 725-0820, Fax: (650) 725-3457

Printed in the United States of America on acid-free, archival-quality paper

Library of Congress Cataloging-in-Publication Data

Names: Wasserman, Noam, 1969– author.

Title: Life is a startup : what founders can teach us about making choices and managing change / Noam Wasserman.

Description: Stanford, California : Stanford Business Books, an imprint of Stanford University Press, 2019. | Includes bibliographical references and index.

Identifiers: LCCN 2018019423 (print) | LCCN 2018023186 (ebook) | ISBN 9781503607422 (electronic) | ISBN 9781503601758 (cloth : alk. paper)

Subjects: LCSH: Success. | Life skills. | Decision making. | Change (Psychology) | Entrepreneurship—Psychological aspects.

Classification: LCC BF637.S8 (ebook) | LCC BF637.S8 W3285 2019 (print) | DDC 658.1/1—dc23

LC record available at https://lccn.loc.gov/2018019423

Designed by Bruce Lundquist

Typeset by Newgen in 10/14 Minion

CONTENTS

LIFE IS A STARTUP

INTRODUCTION

OVER THE PAST TWO DECADES I've pretty much become "the founder guy" in academia and beyond. I've immersed myself in studying the people who begin startups. My course and case studies, my database of twenty thousand entrepreneurs and interviews with hundreds of them, and my book on founders' dilemmas were aimed at teaching people how to build successful startups and founding teams.

My focus suddenly expanded on a warm spring day in 2010. I was in my office on the campus of Harvard Business School when one of the students in my entrepreneurship course came into my office, full of excitement, to tell me that he would probably never start a business. With a startled laugh, I replied, "Sorry that you're taking the wrong course, David!" "Not at all!" he said. "Your course has already changed my marriage!"

After letting that sink in, David explained that he and his wife had been struggling to communicate and make decisions about their next steps. He was nearing graduation, and questions around which of two jobs he should take had quickly evolved into "Who decides which city we live in?" and "Your career is taking priority over mine!" For David and many like him, relationship equality—both partners carrying essentially the same work and family responsibilities—is an assumed necessity. But as David had learned in class, the most effective founders resist the natural pull toward equality, instead giving each collaborator authority over a specific area. David had realized that splitting everything down the middle led to resentment, especially if both parties believed that all major decisions should leave both people equally happy. Now, with responsibilities clarified, communicating with his wife got easier.

Taking another lesson from the successful founders who make a point of having difficult conversations with their cofounders up front, David and his wife were tackling uncomfortable issues head-on and forcing themselves to anticipate challenges they might face. David had seen that rather than take risks as everyone assumes they do, founders identified and managed risks, and he and his wife were now doing the same. All of a sudden, they were more adeptly managing the venture that was their life together.

It was a lightning bolt moment for me. No one had ever extended my lessons to realms outside of founding, and none of the researchers I work with in entrepreneurship or my colleagues in personal change management had ever drawn the dotted line so directly between the two realms. David was right: Whether or not we will be founders, we can all learn profound life lessons from the counterintuitive practices and behaviors of successful entrepreneurs.

I also realized that I had been applying some of the founders' lessons to my own life. Not at first, of course—when I was starting out as a computer engineer, I didn't know much about startups. It wasn't until I founded my own systems-integration practice and then worked with founders as a venture capitalist that I began to experience, observe, and analyze entrepreneurs' best and worst practices. I turned observation and analysis into an academic career, first at Harvard Business School and now at the University of Southern California, where I recently started (yes, founded) a new academic center called Founder Central. As I pursued my academic interest—learning what leads to startup success or failure and developing courses on how to avoid the pitfalls—I discovered many ways to fit founders' strategies into my career decisions, as well as aspects of my twenty-eight-year marriage and the parenting of my six daughters and two sons.

One of the benefits of being an educator is that the classroom allows us to experiment. So I started asking my students to pay closer attention to the deeper lessons in my case studies of entrepreneurs and in the experiential exercises I had developed to train my students to be better founders. For their semester-ending writing assignment, I had them "teach" one founding best practice to someone who could apply the best practice in a career decision, personal relationship, managerial challenge, or other "nonfounding" walk of life. I had lengthy discussions with students and alumni about the challenges they faced in these other areas. Many described how entrepreneurs' exemplary tales had been useful as they came to points in their lives when they feared that their decision making was being skewed by their own blinders or their ability to shift gears was being thwarted by what we called "magnetic pulls" of similarity and equality.

The stories from the people I talked to reinforced my sense of the particular challenges of our age. Roles and expectations are increasingly up for grabs. Whether we freelance or work for large organizations, whether our family involves marriage and kids or something else, it feels as though we each have to find a new roadmap for our journeys.

In other words, life is a startup—and we are the founders of our own lives.

THE INFLECTION POINTS OF LIFE

This book is for people who may never have the name of a startup on their business card but want to be armed for life's inflection points. It is a resource for those who might want to make a change or create a stronger foundation for a new endeavor, whether in their personal or professional lives. It may be particularly valuable for those in the early stages of their careers and in long-term relationships. But the book also offers important advice for anyone contemplating a new endeavor, whether it's switching jobs, moving to a new location, or entering a creative activity. The challenges explored in this book can arise at almost any point in life and for a wide range of people. This includes those who are midstream in their current lives but who are struggling to balance the demands of work with the responsibilities of family while still trying to figure out how to pursue their most cherished dreams. In addition, if you are a founder, this book will help you readily apply to greater effect the hard-knocks lessons you may not know you know.

I draw on numerous sources that hold insights for many of the most important decisions that we face in life. We learn from the direct experiences of a wide range of individuals at different stages of life and career, from young people seeking greater meaning in their jobs to couples pursuing work-life balance to midcareer managers looking to climb out of the corporate rut. I also mine my rich database of nearly twenty thousand entrepreneurs and the insights from my firsthand work with founders like Tim Westergren of Pandora Radio, Evan Williams of Blogger and Twitter, and Hillary Mallow of ProLab. I tap my own founding experiences; my discussions with students, alumni, and others facing a wide range of life dilemmas; and my interviews with past, current, and aspiring entrepreneurs.

As a result, I'm able to go deeply into the entrepreneurial mind-set to investigate the challenges successful entrepreneurs have faced, the counterintuitive thinking that sets them apart, and the relevance of their actions for our life decisions. I don't suggest that all entrepreneurs are paradigms or even that all of them provide valuable examples. Instead, I've gleaned lessons from the smartest moves that I've observed over the course of twenty years. I tap the wisdom of the best at their most effective.

As a professor, I also draw on best-in-class research from a variety of behavioral sciences—including psychology, economics, sociology, and family and gender studies—and the entrepreneurial wisdom in ancient writings, such as the Talmud and the classical work *Ethics of the Fathers*, to outfit you with lessons that are both rigorous and road tested. How have founders learned when to jump into new businesses and when to hold back? What are their secrets about sharing responsibilities, dealing with failure, and planning for success? I explore how their best practices can help each of us make better decisions, solve problems, manage relationships, and achieve growth in both our personal and professional lives.

ENVISIONING CHANGE AND MAKING IT HAPPEN

The book is divided into two parts. Collectively they cover the most important lessons my Founder's Dilemmas course has to offer that are also applicable to nonfounding walks of life. In the first part, I talk about *envisioning change*. Because long before anything occurs, something is happening: problem framing is just as important—if not more—than problem solving! Then, I consider *managing change*: how we can best execute on the plans we envision. Each part includes chapter pairings that address problems and solutions in turn. The first of each duo focuses on the challenges that we face in life, drawing parallels between the personal-life challenge and an equivalent founding challenge. The second focuses on the solutions to those problems: I look at how founders tackle those hurdles and how we can apply their approaches ourselves.

Part I, on envisioning change, begins with a duo of chapters that delve into factors that prevent us from making a desired change and, on the flip side, lead us to make a change too hastily. Some people are *constrained by handcuffs* that they progressively create for themselves. Others get so excited about a change that they become *blinded by passion* and rush in too quickly. We look at how founders overcome their fear of leaping while keeping even their most ardent passions in check and see how we can apply their best practices ourselves.

The next duo of chapters addresses the challenges posed by failure and by success. Our *fear of failure* prevents us from making changes, and when failure occurs, we suffer greatly. On the flip side, we don't appreciate the potential *perils of success*—how achieving our dreams can lead to its own set of problems. These challenges apply to everything from applying for a promotion to contemplating a relocation to planning a radical career move. I look at how founders increase the chances that they will be able to fail well and to anticipate and manage the perils of success.

In Part II, on managing change, I look at decision making and problem solving—the kinds of challenges that arise *after* you have envisioned the change you want to make and are moving into the "doing" phase. We learn from founders the critical importance of thinking ahead despite, and even because of, our temptation to respond reactively to new developments.

First, I examine the risks of relying too heavily on our *blueprints*, or the well-worn personal mental patterns that we use to make choices. I discuss how the best founders tune into the potential disconnects between their existing blueprints and the challenges they are about to face and how they act to reduce those disconnects before they get blindsided by them. For instance, a powerful part of our blueprints is the inclination for birds of a feather to flock together, also known as *homophily*. We are naturally drawn toward collaborators who are similar to us, often to our peril. The best founders have seen the problems caused by this tendency, including heightened tensions due to overlapping capabilities and gaping holes in their teams. Rather than depending on too-similar collaborators, the best founders relentlessly take stock of their own weaknesses and recruit people with skills and viewpoints that differ from their own, even if that makes the founders uncomfortable.

I then turn to two powerful, but problematic, magnetic pulls: the tendency to involve family and close friends in our endeavors, and the allure of equality. I demonstrate why we are playing with fire when we *involve those who are near and dear to us* and how the best entrepreneurs diagnose the areas with the highest potential for blowups, creating firewalls to prevent those blowups. I also discuss the problems caused by the *powerful pull of equality*, both within our teams as we strive for fairness and in egalitarian personal relationships in which we take pride. While effective entrepreneurs have a healthy respect for consensus, they know that an overreliance on building a unified view can prevent progress. In addition to dividing responsibilities and giving each person sole authority over a particular area, they resist the siren song of equality when it comes to splitting ownership among themselves. The reality is that few collaborators—whether cofounders or couples—truly contribute equally, and I show how pretending otherwise can be counterproductive or even destructive.

I conclude with an exploration of a trade-off that most of us face at one point or another: What do we give up when we fight to maintain control, whether in a job, a project, or a relationship? And what do we gain when we yield control? When does it make sense to give up control to get those gains? For insights, I draw on my research into the rich versus king trade-off facing founders: if founders want to get rich from their startups, they can't expect to be the absolute monarch; if they intend to rule single-handedly, they can't expect the startup to reach its full potential, financially and in its impact on the world.

As I cover these topics, I investigate several themes that cut across each and recur again and again: How do founders apply rational thinking to harness and focus their emotions, enabling them to balance head and heart? How do they manage conversations about difficult topics, often with people close to them and with whom they tend to avoid such conversations? And how do they avoid being seduced by short-term gains? Starting a business often requires daily, all-consuming battles for survival—making it all the more impressive to see successful entrepreneurs fight those urgent battles while keeping their eyes on the distant horizon.

Whether you're facing major decisions, an imminent move, or difficulties in a close relationship, these lessons can be applied to the constants of risk, growth, decision making, and problem solving. They can help you make more-informed choices about whether and how to act. My hope is that the lessons of the most effective founders will carry you along through whatever personal venture you launch—and bring you an outcome you will celebrate.

PART I

ENVISIONING A CHANGE

CHAPTER 1

THE FUTURE CALLS

Do You Answer?

VISIONS OF WHAT WE MIGHT someday achieve, or who we might someday become, often serve as sources of inspiration. However, when it comes to taking action, we divide into distinct groups.

Most of us, convinced of the impracticality of making a leap into the unknown, eventually give up any hope that we'll pursue our cherished ideas. Those ideas become fantasies of the past, reflected on and maybe even pined over as we go about our "real" lives. At the other end of the spectrum, others remain so enraptured by a goal that—at some point—they act on impulse, tear themselves from the mundane, and go for it, come what may.

We all need to nourish our dreams. Giving up on them is a recipe for emptiness and a lot of regret. But plunging headlong can result in a concussion. Over the next four chapters, I consider both of these problematic extremes and the gray area between them. Even though they are in some ways opposite and tend to be faced by very different kinds of people, they arise from a common root: Sometimes, we unthinkingly follow injurious, though natural, inclinations instead of seeking to understand and counteract them.

Those who start companies—founders—are sometimes good role models for overcoming these particular problems: they're practiced at seeing all the dimensions of the opportunity landscape, including, most significantly, the dimension of time. In anticipation of becoming entrepreneurs, the best of them prepare themselves for the ultimate leap–no leap decision. They scan the foreseeable future for obstacles. They keep their eyes on the potential future rewards. Many of these adept individuals have shuffled through my office over the years. But so too have young people and executives who struggle with life changes. Consider Caroline and Akhil, whose characteristics embody those who struggle with changes. Caroline is a person who can't leap into a new life situation, and Akhil is too quick to rush in. Their stories help us examine the two biggest problems we face in terms of taking risks well: succumbing to the incremental tightening of handcuffs, both financial and psychic, and blindly following our passions.

CONTEMPLATING A LEAP

Caroline, now nearing thirty, carefully planned her career so that she could have it all: a compelling résumé, a reasonable lifestyle, and, eventually, real fulfillment in her job—just like we all hope to have.

In the final months of business school, she debated with herself about what kind of job to take. She had always wanted to do something in social enterprise, preferably involving special needs because of the challenges faced by her sister who has autism. But, as she put out feelers, she realized that it would be many years before she'd be able to pay off her MBA debt and buy a house if she simply followed her dream. Instead, she opted to return to a job in finance, which offered intellectual challenge, a clear career trajectory, and financial security. It justified the tuition and the two years of income she had invested to achieve her degree.

As several of her friends had pointed out, it wasn't an either-or decision: She could gain more work experience, build up a cash cushion, and then venture into something in social enterprise. She really could have everything she wanted—someday.

Tapping her signing bonus, Caroline and her husband bought a Victorian-style home in a Boston suburb with a strong school district. It came with a hefty mortgage that put Caroline on edge. However, her parents told her that you should always buy as much house as you can afford, and she felt more comfortable after several housewarming parties showed that friends had made the same choice. Right on schedule, she and her husband had their first child, Eva, and hired a full-time nanny so that Caroline could return to work. Childcare was surprisingly expensive, but as friends said, once you found a system that worked, you would pay almost anything to maintain it.

A good part of Caroline's pay consists of deferred compensation that she gets over time as she stays longer and longer. After all, as she becomes more valuable to her firm, they want to provide incentive for her to stay, or at least for her to think twice about what she's giving up if she ever thinks about leaving.[1] As her career progresses, her paychecks get bigger, although her disposable income has actually shrunk, thanks to her high-cost lifestyle.

Now, after a few years, she has become disillusioned with her job, which requires long hours and is dominated by the firm's strict hierarchy. She realizes it will be a long time before she gets significant responsibility. She sees Eva very little. Even though she is financially at ease, she doesn't feel the peace of mind or sense of accomplishment that she thought stability would bring.

She is tempted to change jobs but fears that her deep focus on a single industry has begun limiting her ability to shift to another, more dynamic industry or to one in which she can take on a larger role. Caroline is realizing that, as she tells me, "my focus has become a ball and chain, preventing a move into a new realm." An article she read in her alumni magazine has increased her anxiety. The article described research into MBA students who develop a tight, consistent focus on a specific career yet receive fewer job offers and significantly lower compensation offers than students whose backgrounds are less focused.[2] (The same effect is also found in a very different industry, professional sports. Even after accounting for their other contributions to the team, specialist basketball players, such as those who focus on three-point shooting, have historically tended to have lower compensation and fan appeal than generalist players.[3])

One afternoon Caroline runs into a former classmate who went straight from business school into a nonprofit that runs ski schools for disabled children at New England winter resorts. She hears her classmate's enthusiasm about the nonprofit and feels a pang of regret. But she also experiences a jolt of inspiration. The adaptive-skiing concept reminds her that she and her sister were avid horseback riders and that her sister seemed to light up whenever she was around horses. Could she work instead for an organization that teaches horseback riding to children with autism or something similar?

The more the idea takes shape in her mind, the more daunting the details seem. She'd probably have to learn a lot about the field. Her only experiences with autism are personal. She'd undoubtedly have to take a pay cut and might have to move. There would be risk and sacrifice. Caroline knows that, at this point in their lives, neither she nor her husband wants to forfeit their nice house and neighborhood. Nor could they do without her sizable income supporting their equally sizable outflow to keep the gears of their current setup turning. The spending rate—her personal "burn rate," to adapt a term for the amount startups spend—seems like an inextricable barrier to her personal freedom.

Caroline has suddenly discovered that she's wearing *handcuffs*: inducements or penalties that increase the cost of change and thus dissuade us from shifting gears in ways we would otherwise find attractive. As we see in this chapter and the next one, they come in many forms and are often of our own making. Long ago, Caroline made decisions that seemed right at the time; she even seemed to be achieving important aspirations, such as owning a home. But these choices later constrained her decision making, thanks, for instance, to the high-cost mortgage and the nanny she had taken on. She has found that the incremental decisions she thought were merely fulfilling her immediate needs have put her dream career in jeopardy.

Put another way, the same thing that happens to all of us has happened to Caroline: We make decisions that make sense each step of the way, but, as a result, change becomes increasingly costly over time, challenging any major break from the status quo.

With her mortgage and the family's enjoyment of their large home, Caroline's decisions have led to imprisonment in a golden palace. At work, her deferred compensation and the high salary she is enjoying and spending have locked golden handcuffs onto her wrists.

Caroline's story isn't unique. In a very different realm, retired Royal Australian Air Force air commodore and researcher M. J. Rawlinson studied Australian air force technicians in their late thirties and early forties who were within a few years of achieving their pension benefit, due after twenty years of service.[4] Many of them were highly dissatisfied with their jobs. Yet these golden handcuffs kept most of them from leaving early.[5]

This isn't true only for technicians who might have been underpaid and likely needed the retirement money; individuals at other end of the wealth spectrum also fall prey to the financial inducements of golden handcuffs. New York University finance professors Rangarajan Sundaram and David Yermack reviewed compensation for 237 Fortune 500 companies between 1996 and 2002. Fortune 500 CEOs—already worth millions—became much more likely to retire after their pensions became fully payable.[6] These wealthy executives probably did not think that their preferred term as CEO would be affected by the pension vesting schedule determined by their boards of directors! In principle, they were already millionaires and could do what they pleased. But the handcuffs kept them in place.

You might expect this outcome in ritualized fields like finance and the military or any highly structured corporation. But the same applies in the entrepreneurial realm, which has a reputation of being far more fast and loose. Author Randall Stross was granted an impressive amount of access to the internal operations and thought processes of the team that runs Y Combinator, a prominent startup incubator. He captured their perspective on the founders they were evaluating: "If there is a single perfect age for founders to start a startup, [it is when they are] a little more mature than undergraduate students but not yet encumbered with the mortgages and children that make leaving a conventional, well-paying job at an established, profitable company so difficult."[7]

However, handcuffs aren't only golden but also social and emotional. Sociologist Howard Becker of Northwestern University showed that the secondary aspects of a job can unexpectedly come to constrain behavior.[8] For instance, a person might initially take a job primarily for the high income but later resist moving to an even higher-paying job elsewhere because of an unexpected, secondary aspect of the job—some variable the person hadn't even considered when first taking the position, such as a friendship with a new coworker or enjoyment of the unexpectedly convenient commute. We rarely take a job with those aspects driving the decision, but the handcuffs caused by them can often prevent us from leaving.

Caroline's handcuffs tightened slowly, imperceptibly, as she moved from her previous job to business school, married, took her present job, became a mother, and accumulated assets. Each of these actions embedded her in her current communities, socially and emotionally. These nonfinancial handcuffs often include positive ties that keep us put: appreciation and loyalty, a strong support network, potential promotions, prestige, and the list could go on.

Investment banker Dilip Rao was an executive MBA student in my Founder's Dilemmas course. His experiences highlight these psychic handcuffs in thinking about his own trajectory. Rao had originally planned to go to medical school, but his family's financial problems prevented him from doing so. Instead, he got a job at financial-services firm Credit Suisse. He told me:

> I was determined to pursue a career in finance. I had read inspiring stories
> about great CEOs like Sidney Weinberg. He had no formal education prior to

Wall Street, came from poverty, and his background contrasted greatly with that of the traditional Ivy League Wall Street guy. There was something gritty about Wall Street—and if Mr. Weinberg could work his way up from a janitor's assistant to the longest-serving CEO of Goldman Sachs, and . . . others who had no business getting a job on Wall Street had done so in the face of desperation, turmoil, and insurmountable hardships, what was my excuse? It was August 2007; I had three other mouths, plus a dog, to feed and a roof to keep over our heads.

During his first three years at Credit Suisse, he was able to get his family onto much more solid financial footing. At that point, many of his colleagues were planning the next stages of their lives, and Rao began to feel the itch to do something more entrepreneurial. However, he also felt a deep sense of loyalty to the firm:

> They took a chance on me and gave me the opportunity to prove myself. More importantly, my job enabled me to take care of my family at my time of most need. I owed a sense of loyalty to people I had worked with and for. They had taken me under their wing and taught me everything I knew. For the first time in my life, there were people that I wasn't related to who took a personal interest in my life and invested in me. The only way I could show those people how thankful I am was to keep working for them and to work incredibly hard.

He ended up working for Credit Suisse for eight years, far longer than originally expected. His comfort in the firm complemented his sense of loyalty:

> You spend time at any given place and immerse 100 percent of yourself in your craft, and you become a known entity. You know who to call to get things done, and, most importantly, you have a brand; when that brand is associated with work ethic and trustworthiness, it only compounds every year. More importantly, with that brand and time invested into the firm comes the ability to influence, which is incredibly powerful in terms of social capital and goodwill. Every two years or so, I've had an opportunity to leave Credit Suisse for another position, but it is really hard to walk away from the years of goodwill I have generated.

Reinforcing this was the series of potential promotions that loomed each year. As Rao observed: "I kept feeling like I could get to the next level each year. My boss said, 'You're on a great trajectory, making great revenue for the firm, a leader here—you'll get fast-tracked, be able to run a business.' I believed it, so I put off the planning for what to do next."

The handcuffs of working in a prestigious industry or firm can be quite powerful. I first observed the handcuffs of prestige when a Harvard Business School colleague—who prided himself on being a "3H person," with three degrees from Harvard—decided not to pursue a very attractive, high-impact role at another school in part because of the prestige of the Harvard name and the halo of having a tenured position there. Instead, a more junior colleague who wasn't as bound by those handcuffs took the position. A year into her new position, the more junior colleague was much happier than I remember the senior colleague ever being at Harvard. Harvard's school colors are crimson and gold. The school's powerful crimson handcuffs of prestige are well known for tying people to the school even when a better opportunity (and more gold?) beckons elsewhere.

You've probably noticed your own handcuffs if you've contemplated such things as jumping to a new company, relocating for an existing job, or even applying for a promotion. Such handcuffs also exist in the personal realm. For instance, the comforts of a long-term relationship with a significant other can impose similar handcuffs. Observing this, one of my students said: "Those who are unhappy sometimes stay because they experience 'handcuffs' that make them scared of leaving. They stay in unfulfilling relationships because of powerful secondary gains like security, safety, and predictability. Why leave that person and risk the unknown, right?" Likewise, moving to a new city creates the need to cultivate a new circle of friends, to learn new routes to the store and restaurants, and to develop new routines to replace our comfortable old ones.

It's true, of course, that handcuffs can prevent unwise actions. Sometimes we're thankful in retrospect that we weren't swayed by the advice to follow our passions wherever they lead. (We consider that shortly.) It's also true that appreciation and loyalty are wonderful attributes and habits to inculcate in ourselves and in those around us. But, too often, our handcuffs hold us back from pursuing good ideas that might lead to greater fulfillment.

The tightness of handcuffs feels very real. And certainly there's nothing more real than the need to make a mortgage payment or the need for a secure home. But it's easy to lose sight of the role played by perception, especially when we feel a sense of urgency.[9] If we step away from the seeming urgency of remaining in our current place, we can see that the handcuffs represent nothing more than a series of incremental decisions that individually seemed to make sense at the time they were made. They represent the reactive part of you, the side that diligently responds to the need to earn money, be secure, educate your children, and so on, that takes you down a particular course one day at a time. But there's another part of you—the proactive part—that is capable of thinking beyond your immediate exigencies and imagining a future.

Most of us tend to rely on the reactive to the point where we neglect the proactive. We come to think of the handcuffs as not only hampering our immediate actions but also circumscribing our entire world.

Caroline's professional handcuffs of perfection can also become an obstacle when dating, akin to a potential founder who keeps waiting for the perfect idea to emerge. For example, dating-advice columnist Evan Mark Katz talks about how he helped a twice-divorced sixty-something woman start dating again. Before long she had several compelling options, but she continued to hesitate. "He's not the rugged type." "We're the same height, and I like to wear boots." Katz's advice for romantic maximizers like his client: give the almost-perfect candidate a chance.[10]

Data on first marriages appear to back up Katz's approach. A study by Nicholas Wolfinger, a sociologist at the University of Utah, explored the best age to get married. He found that the risk of divorce for first marriage declines steadily from one's teens into midtwenties and then begins to climb again in one's thirties. Past the age of thirty-two, the odds of divorce climb by 5 percent a year.[11] Wolfinger notes that this increase in divorce rate is a relatively recent phenomenon and underscores that this effect remains in place even after controlling for a variety of variables, including sex, race, the family structure in which one grew up, and metropolitan area of residence. Wolfinger believes that a selection effect is in play, explaining that those most predisposed to succeed at marriage tend to marry in their twenties, leaving a smaller pool of attractive candidates later in life.

Let's pause for a moment and reflect on Caroline's situation and possibly our own. Caroline's source of freedom—her high income—has become a very real source of constraint. As we see in the next chapter, there are concrete ways to reactively deal with these constraints. However, proactively diagnosing the sources of our potential constraints can open up far better options for avoiding or weakening the handcuffs in advance.

Pause for Reflection

To set the table for our exploration in the next chapter of founders' solutions to these problems, and to explore their relevance for solving similar challenges in our own lives, ask yourself:

- If you were Caroline, handcuffed but seeking greater fulfillment by making a change, what would be your inclination at this point?

- In your own life, have you ever faced an important decision in which you were not able to pursue your preferred choice because of personal or professional constraints? If you had been aware of those constraints a year or two (or five) earlier, could you have proactively reduced or removed them?

- Are there decisions you might face a year or two from now that could pose a similar challenge? Think through how your constraints might continue to affect your decisions. Are there things you can do now to make your preferred choice more viable?

THE DANGERS OF UNBRIDLED PASSIONS

When we ask these questions of ourselves, we're trying to check our tendency to avoid risk by replacing it with an easier path to future rewards. But we may also be trying to contend with another urge: the tendency to dive in headlong, chasing what we think is our passion without an understanding of the consequences. When people move impetuously into entrepreneurial ventures, it's often because they have an unformed view of the preparation required.[12] Sometimes it's because they have an exaggerated sense of urgency. A morbid dread of showing up late to market or being beaten by the competition can get entrepreneurs into trouble. Friendster was the first major social-networking site, debuting a year before MySpace and two years before Facebook. However, in its push to attract users, Friendster overestimated its ability to handle them.[13] The site slowed considerably, sparking users' desire to try out its emerging competitors. When we dive into any important endeavor in life without thinking twice, we heighten the risk that our passion will become our undoing.

Let's meet Akhil, an engineering school graduate. In temperament and interests, he couldn't be more different from Caroline. Akhil's cleantech startup had just made it to the final round of a new-venture competition (top prize: $25,000) when he got a voicemail. It was from a human-resources executive at the technology company that had offered him an excellent job months before.

"Akhil, we are finally ready to ramp up the division, and I can't hold your position open much longer," the executive said. "We know that you'll be a terrific addition to the team, and we love your passion for our work. However, we need an answer. We need to hear back within the next two weeks, or we will go on to the next candidate."

The firm was developing a new line of cleantech services—the industry about which Akhil has long been passionate. He was assured that if he took the job, he and his fiancée, Roopa, would be able to move back home to India, where he would help launch the Mumbai office—a challenging, entrepreneurial assignment. His entire family pushed for him to take the offer, and Roopa agreed. She viewed the job as the best route to the couple's financial security. She also envisioned starting their family in India and didn't want to delay too long.

But there's that startup. Akhil hasn't been as excited by anything like it in his professional life. It was *colpo di fulmine*—an Italian phrase that likens passion to a thunderbolt, one that cracks your chest open, changing you forever. At this moment, Akhil is smitten with his startup, especially given its showing in the new-venture competition. "I don't think I've ever been this excited!" he thought. "The fact that I am making this thing a reality, it's like a straight shot of adrenaline to my veins!" His commitment to getting it off the ground, whatever the risks, is understandable. Like peers of his vintage, he has constantly heard that he should follow his passions. "However," he said, "Roopa will have to be on board. I will need her support if I'm to see this through. I just have to figure out how to convince her. She's concerned about our financial stability, especially the loans we're taking out to pay for grad school, and how that will affect our ability to start a family." He summons all of his entrepreneurial charm and persuades Roopa that, within a year, the startup will be able to raise outside funding, providing the financial stability she craves. He turns down the job offer.

In doing so, he falls into a trap that has claimed too many entrepreneurs: Enthusiasm blinds them to reality. In a study led by Arnold C. Cooper of Purdue University, three thousand small-business owners put their own firms' odds of success at the equivalent of 81 percent on average but other, similar companies' odds at just 59 percent.[14] Overestimation of our company's prospects is compounded by overestimation of our own abilities in an unfamiliar context.

This is a human pattern, not just an entrepreneurial one. An unexpectedly high percentage of people suffer from the same bias. Neuroscientist Tali Sharot reports that 80 percent of the population display an *optimism bias* that leads us to underestimate the probability of negative events occurring and overestimate the probability of positive events occurring.[15] For instance, we underestimate the probability of our getting divorced and overestimate the chances that our children will be very talented. We underestimate the probability of being in a car accident and overestimate our chances of success on the job market. People with high optimism are more likely to smoke and less likely to save money, undergo recommended medical screenings, and buy insurance. The bias is found across all genders, races, nationalities, and ages. It is so powerful that expertise is often insufficient to counter it: "Divorce lawyers underestimate the negative consequences of divorce, financial analysts expect improbably high profits, and medical doctors overestimate the effectiveness of their treatment."[16]

Akhil, clouded by his passion, was misreading his chances of getting outside financing. Every day he felt as though the business was just about to gain traction, yet he couldn't attract capital. The year came and went. Roopa, afraid of deflating his dream, kept silent, but her resentment grew. "Nothing that Akhil promised me has worked out," she said to a trusted friend. "We're already in so much debt as it is. Why doesn't he see what's really important here?"

Akhil's original campaign "to convince her to support me"—to *sell, sell, sell* Roopa on the idea of the startup—has prevented him from productively handling a pivotal, difficult conversation. Instead of building a robust foundation of support that could withstand the inevitable storms, Akhil's overly persuasive approach built a very fragile foundation. Unlike Caroline, he's not locked into a lifestyle that keeps him on a corporate treadmill, but his passion has harmed rather than honed his situation. His relationship with Roopa has suffered, and they've delayed their personal desires—a big wedding, a move home to India, and the start of their own family. It's a mistake that often dooms a startup, as it would any other initiative dependent on constituents' moral support.

It's easy to smile (or grimace) and shake our heads knowingly at Akhil's mistakes. But his is a familiar story. Sometimes our passions are so strong that they overcome even public pushback from the people who mean the most to us. Consider Luke Walton of the National Basketball Association (NBA). While playing in the league as a reserve for nearly a decade, he had developed a reputation for hard work. After retiring in 2013, he began exploring a next career as a coach, quickly working his way up from assistant coach at the University of Memphis to player-development coach of a team in the NBA's Development League. Soon after, he reached the pinnacle of the sport, hired by the NBA's Golden State Warriors—who were on their way to winning the league's championship in 2015—as an assistant coach.

Before the next season, the team's head coach, Steve Kerr, suffered from excruciating back problems, and Walton was named interim head coach. Under his leadership, the team got off to the fastest start in history. When the team beat the Los Angeles Lakers in November for its sixteenth win, it broke the league record for consecutive victories to start a season. The team extended the record to twenty-four games before losing, and was 39–4 when Kerr returned to the head-coaching position.

Rumors began spreading about other teams' interest in hiring Walton as head coach. Many of the worst teams in the league—the ones most likely to replace their coaches—were rumored to be seriously considering him to become their comeback kid. In April 2016, rumors intensified that the Lakers, who were on their way to having the worst record in the Western Conference—a remarkable fifty-six games behind Walton's Golden State Warriors—were in hot pursuit of Walton.

Toward the end of April, Walton's father, Bill Walton, who himself had been a star in the NBA for many years and had won two championships as a player, was asked about what his son should do. "Stay where he is!" the senior Walton urged. "Head coaching jobs are open for a reason. What he has right now, it doesn't get any better than that. Money cannot buy what they have on the Warriors right now. I've been on some of the most special teams in the history of basketball: UCLA, Portland, and the Celtics. I have seen the other end of the spectrum too, and so I know. It's so fragile; it's so tenuous."[17]

Yet, on April 29, the Lakers announced that Luke Walton had been hired as their head coach. His first year leading the team, they lost 68 percent of their games; out of the thirty teams in the NBA, only two were worse. Golden State, in contrast, won the league championship for the second time in three years. In the coming years, many eyes will be watching to see whether Luke Walton's confident pursuit of his passion turns into magic or whether discounting his Golden State situation (and his father's public exhortations) leaves him in a lurch like Akhil.

The tendency to leap first and assess afterward pervades many parts of our lives. A surprisingly large number of us do exactly this when we approach the momentous change of getting married. For instance, a survey of one thousand American newlyweds found that 40 percent didn't know their spouse's credit score, one-third were surprised by their spouse's spending habits, and one-third didn't know the amount of their spouse's student loan debt. Some respondents even had secret financial accounts that they hid from their spouses, 61 percent of them men and 39 percent of them women.[18] Passion blinds, causing us to take shortcuts and ignore that which we do not want to see.

Pause for Reflection

If you, like Akhil, might fall prey to unbridled passion, take a moment to reflect on previous times that you allowed desire to guide you and whether that caused errors in your thinking.

- In the past, when you've been passionate about something new, how realistic were your original expectations about the fulfillment it would bring and how much it would cost you?

- When you tried explaining the project or prospect to your significant other or family, did you describe only the project's positive aspects and potential outcomes, or did you also describe some of the pitfalls that might emerge?

    - If the former, think about why you resisted describing the dark side. Did you avoid having a difficult conversation that would have brought to light negative aspects of the situation?

    - In hindsight, do you think describing both the positives and the pitfalls to your inner circle might have boosted their support for your idea, or would it have deflated their support? Why or why not?

SHOULD YOU DIVE IN?

The ultimate entrepreneur—in life and business—is one who combines the passion of the evangelist with the clear thinking of the analyst. However, few people innately combine these often-contradictory attributes. Instead, one or the other is likely to bias our decision making, to our detriment.

We can compare this to someone diving into an unfamiliar pool. The passionate diver will charge up the diving board and leap, without looking to see if there's any water in the pool, whether the diving board is far higher than any she's ever used before, and even whether she is still wearing street clothes. The analyst won't even approach the diving board until she's measured the water to be certain it's the right temperature (to within a tenth of a degree), ensured that the diving board is no taller than the highest one she's ever used, and secured not only a bathing suit but also scuba gear.

The overpassionate diver will be likely to regret rash decisions that lead to broken bones. The overcautious diver will be likely to regret never challenging herself to live her dreams and find a swimming stroke at which she could excel. However, with more awareness of their own tendencies and the ways to counteract their negative effects, each can achieve a better dive, actual or metaphorical. How can they do so? By adopting the best practices of founders. With the likely challenges of our mind-sets laid out before us, that is what we tackle next.

CHAPTER 2

YOUR BEST ANSWER

How to Move Forward

IN THIS CHAPTER I tap the best practices used by a variety of founders and entrepreneurially minded folks to help us prepare for our desired changes. As I have studied and worked with entrepreneurs, I've shaped my research into a set of basic guidelines for the challenges that they face while founding. That same advice applies to other walks of life. Here I first tackle how best to escape from the handcuffs that prevent us from making changes. Then I provide lessons about channeling our passions in productive ways that won't lead us to jump too soon.

BREAK YOUR HANDCUFFS

Some handcuffs are obvious—making them easy to plan for—but many of the most important are not. For instance, when planning for change, it's easier to anticipate the financial challenges we might face than the psychological challenges that await us. Psychic handcuffs are usually far more devious, being harder to see (or even admit) and having fewer clear solutions. With both types of handcuffs, though, we often find it hard to summon the discipline to avoid them—much like Dilip and Caroline in Chapter 1—until it is too late. The best practices of founders suggest proactive steps we can take to reduce or break our handcuffs, progressively loosening them instead of letting them continually tighten around our wrists.

Reduce Your Personal Burn Rate

After getting an MBA, Christina took a job with a consulting firm in New York. Before grad school she had worked for a nonprofit and been paid accordingly, so it was understandable that she viewed the new job as her long-awaited opportunity to achieve a more comfortable standard of living. However, having learned from Caroline's regrets in my course, Christina fought that inclination. "I knew going into consulting that it was a temporary thing, not a forever thing, and I didn't want to get used to that lifestyle," she told me. A financial cushion would give Christina a sense of security and the option to leave for a lower-paying job if she wanted. And so she began by finding ways to stash money away. For instance, despite living in Manhattan, one of the most costly cities in the country, she limited herself to renting a small apartment that cost $1,350 a month. She aggressively kept herself from digging deeper into debt while finding creative ways to live cheaply, like taking advantage of the free food that came with attending parties and going on dates.

Christina first focused on proactively managing student debt. Research from the Federal Reserve Bank of Philadelphia shows that when prospective entrepreneurs are burdened with debt payments, they lack the cash cushion to start a business. One standard-deviation increase in student debt within a zip code resulted in a 25 percent decrease in the number of nascent businesses with one to five employees.[1] Translated to daily life, this means debt can be a real handcuff. Coming out of school, Christina aggressively paid down her loans. Rather than spending her signing bonus on travel or furnishings for an apartment, as many of her classmates did, she made a big payment on her loans. Her actions got even more aggressive two years later when Christina cofounded a clothing company. "Another founder told us about how she stopped paying her student loans when she founded her startup," Christina said. "The logic made sense: If our startup succeeded, it wouldn't matter that we racked up a little extra interest over the year or two we were in forbearance, and if it failed, that extra cash flow meant we gave it everything we had." But Christina paid her loans as aggressively as possible for as long as she could: up to four months before her company's launch, she was paying three to four times the minimum monthly payment.

Why take this approach when Christina was working so hard, first as a consultant and then as a founder? Every raise feels comfortable much more quickly than we realize, and we get locked into golden handcuffs even if we think we won't. Between her cost consciousness, paying down of debt, and active saving, Christina was effectively living on the same post-MBA salary as she had pre-

MBA. But she had future freedom. Each step of the way, Christina asked herself: Is the added comfort from spending this now worth tighter constraints later?

When the time came to give up her consulting paycheck and found the business, she says, "I moved from my apartment that cost $1,350 a month onto a couch on the Upper West Side of Manhattan that cost me $400 a month." Each night she had to fold up the couch and conceal any signs of her presence in the living room by hiding clothes on book shelves and shoes in kitchen cabinets. "I had also maxed out my frequent-flyer rewards points at my consulting job, which enabled my cofounder and me to cover our travel for the first year or so of our startup."

She had realized that the biggest issue most entrepreneurs face when leaping is loss of income. To prevent an eventual cash-flow crunch, she lived like a founder before she actually had to. When she wasn't taking advantage of the food at parties or while on dates, she "ate on five dollars a day, which in New York City gets you a coffee and a falafel."

Ryan Broyles's compensation was far higher than Christina's, yet he also harnessed worries about future constraints to take a similar approach. Broyles was a National Football League player who resisted the lavish lifestyles of his peers by forcing himself to live on $60,000 a year despite making ten times that amount.[2] His triggers for doing so? Data he had seen showed how short NFL careers are, and personal experience drove home the fact that he was one injury away from losing his paycheck. (The most effective motivator is often the fact that you learned a painful lesson firsthand, as Broyles had from past injuries.) Harnessing secondhand lessons by using the data on career lengths to reinforce his motivation was much less painful.

Summoning the discipline to do this is often quite hard when one's salary and resources are plentiful. But, like Christina and Ryan, great founders also resist the social pressure to buy the nicest house they can afford; instead, they keep renting or buy a less-impressive home than what they could afford. They enforce frugality with automatic mechanisms to divert money each month to a savings account. With savings from a low personal burn rate, founders are able to keep the startup's lights on another day (or year) and to give themselves and their family confidence that they won't be squeezed if the startup takes twice as long and costs twice as much to develop.

The earlier you take these steps, the better. It's far harder to break off handcuffs that have already started tightening around your wrists than to avoid letting them be placed there to begin with. (If only Caroline had looked at homes she could have afforded *after* an enforced monthly savings draw!) Even if you don't have a clear next career step, the same critical steps of constraining spending and reducing debt are needed if you want to be able to take a dream job in a lower-paying industry or want to return to school.

There are concrete things you can do to loosen the wide variety of financial limitations holding you back from pursuing your deepest interests, especially if that interest either requires you to accept a decrease in compensation or requires an investment of your own capital (or both). Focus on the points in life when you have the potential to make a significant change to your personal burn rate, such as when you leave the life of a student and move into the workforce or when you move into a higher-paying position. Recognize that once you get used to the higher-priced lifestyle, it will be far harder to go back to the burn rate of a student than if you fight to remain at that burn rate now. Calculate how much additional money will be coming in and enroll in your brokerage's automatic-investment program in which each month it automatically transfers that amount (or a high percentage of it) into your investment account. Resolve to save every bonus that comes in rather than spending it, starting with your employer's pregraduation signing bonus.

Among the founders who have attended my workshops, 39 percent said that to help them transition to startup life, they had proactively reduced their rate of spending so they could have a bigger cash cushion in the startup. Another 11 percent had moved into a smaller house or apartment before launching their startup. Indeed, on the debt side of our financial obligations, most folks' largest debt-funded outlay is on a house. Instead of stretching to buy the nicest house you can afford, stay disciplined. It should be harder to swallow a hefty monthly mortgage payment if you realize that it's not only money you'll be spending but career freedom as well.

The benefits of living within your means will be twofold: You'll avoid the rude adjustment to a lower standard of living that can act as handcuffs, and you will have saved the cash cushion necessary to buy you the time and stability to explore or make a change (or even to just retire in much better shape than if you hadn't summoned this financial discipline years before). With relatively little investment, you will have bought yourself an option that might become invaluable.

Loosen Your Psychic Handcuffs

However powerful money is, psychic handcuffs can be even more so. If your envisioned leap involves moving, let's say, you may face loss of proximity to friends and family or separation from religious or civic institutions that provide social support. If it entails striking out on your own, you might face a loss of status or managerial responsibility, as well as loss of the comfort of knowing what you're supposed to do every day. You might face an environment in which your existing expertise doesn't count for much. Or you may be looking at a lack of supportive industry resources, such as connections to potential corporate partners or suppliers. Closer to home, you may have to deal with the objections of your spouse or other family members.

Entrepreneurs face these kinds of issues every day. Consider Andrea, a young Denver native who really enjoys skiing, her job as a computer programmer, and proximity to family. However, she came up with a great startup idea in the mobile-advertising arena and worries that to pursue it fully, she would need to quit her job to focus on the idea full time. She would also want to move to startup hub Silicon Valley to gain access to financing and talent. When thinking through such a large transition, though, Andrea hesitates. She tells my research assistant: "Moving will put me far away from my whole family, who are all nearby now. I also have a huge network of connections from when I was at the University of Colorado and from working here in Denver for the past decade. That feels like a lot to give up at this stage of my life to essentially start over somewhere else, even if I know this idea is great!"

When we evaluate a potential leap, we often focus on what we will lose by making the change: lower salary, less prestige, lower rank, and the like. Devote at least as much attention to the potential gains as you do to the losses. Also take a step back, and reflect on the fact that your perceived losses may in part be merely perceptual. Ask yourself how real they are. For example, might your current employer's prestige be keeping you from taking a higher-impact position at a lower-status company?

I was personally handcuffed by this issue when I had the opportunity to leave the Harvard Business School for a much higher-impact role at another school, after spending nearly two decades at Harvard. I knew of several colleagues for whom those Harvard-crimson handcuffs were too hard to break. Reflecting on the lessons from my own course and research—and even planning to write this book—helped me see the handcuffs for what they were and envision a transition. Even so, I found that I needed to progressively shift my identity and mind-set in order to seriously consider other options.

For instance, I sought opportunities to teach at other universities, spending time as a visiting professor at three other schools before formally separating from Harvard. I gave up my office on campus a year before I had to—likewise for giving up the concise "noam@hbs.edu" e-mail address I had always loved using—and stopped attending faculty meetings as soon as possible. Even something as small as changing the signature at the bottom of my e-mails helped free me from the handcuffs and shift my identity away from the school. I started deemphasizing my Harvard affiliation and emphasizing my affiliation with each school at which I was a visiting professor.

I also began focusing less on the school's ranking in the business-school sweepstakes and more on the higher-impact role I would have at a new school. Instead of being yet another full-time Harvard Business School professor among two hundred others, I would be founding director of a new center that would be the first of its kind in the country, or the first business-school researcher among a bunch of engineering professors, in charge of creating a brand-new entrepreneurship curriculum. I learned to appreciate a more entrepreneurial and collaborative culture instead of the more siloed one I was used to.

Also pivotal was a lucrative request I received in the middle of the process to come speak to a large entrepreneurship group. I had always assumed that the interest in my giving those talks was fostered by my association with Harvard. Figuring I would lose this opportunity, but wanting the requester to be fully informed, I answered that I was transitioning out of Harvard and that they should find another of my old colleagues to give the talk. Their answer: We want you, regardless of your affiliation. That reply helped me finally see that I had outgrown my need for a crimson affiliation, or maybe had overestimated its power to begin with. Harvard excels at convincing people—both inside and outside the university—that it epitomizes academic perfection, but a closer look revealed a better fit for me elsewhere.

Escape the Handcuffs of Perfection

Our natural aversion to change can lead us to defer any change that isn't perfect. We let the enemy of the perfect solution be to do nothing. We are handcuffed by hope that we will indeed encounter the perfect situation. For instance, many people avoid working out unless they can do a full workout at the gym. I am no exception when it comes to my preferred forty minutes on a stationary bike—better than a jog during a Boston blizzard and a nice way to make sure I get at least forty minutes of reading done each day. Heaven forbid that I have only thirty minutes free and then have to fight my inclination to bypass the workout! Yet even three minutes of intense intermittent exercise can yield important improvements in health.[3] Though some exercise is much better than none, our handcuffs often lead us to do nothing.

A related type of perfection that can hamper us is the need to bring our projects to complete fruition. One of my students wrote that his biggest "failure fear," which often stops him from getting started on things, is the fear of not finishing—that is, starting something but not putting enough time into it to get to an outcome.

Don't condemn yourself in advance for failing to finish a big task, much as my student with the "failure fear" was likely to do and thus wouldn't even attempt to start the task. I remember a conversation I had with Jan Rivkin, one of Harvard Business School's all-time best teachers and one of its deepest thinkers about pedagogical design. Rivkin had just been asked to take over the school's core strategy course, which had not been doing well. While Rivkin and I were discussing possible ways to tackle the course's steep challenges, he pointed to a quotation he had written on his whiteboard that was taken from the ancient work *Ethics of the Fathers*: "Rabbi Tarfon says: It is not incumbent upon you to finish the task, but neither are you free to desist from it." I hope my student has written the same thing on his whiteboard as a reminder that he shouldn't let his worries about completing a project prevent him from starting. To psych yourself up for a long, grueling race, sometimes it's better to focus on just the first lap or the first hill rather than try to envision the distant finish line and thus not even start. Founders have a term for that approach: *staging*.

Gain Strength Through Staging

A couple of decades ago, standard engineering practice on complex, uncertain projects was to plan, plan, plan; then write, write, write; then hand pages of instructions to armies of implementers; and then sit back and wait for them to code, code, code, or to build, build, build. (This was part of my own upbringing as an engineer.) Then in the early years of the twenty-first century, American engineers borrowed the Japanese concept of lean manufacturing to develop the idea of the "lean startup."[4] Today it's standard practice in tech startups to move forward in short stages—to plan, write, experiment, get feedback, revise, experiment some more, get more feedback, and so on. Successful experiments receive further resources and attention; unsuccessful experiments are abandoned, and the resources and attention are redeployed to other efforts. This staged approach is also used by startup investors, who stage their investments much as startups stage product development.[5] The concept is so compelling, and has been so successful for new ventures, that it has spread to big corporations and military organizations.

This approach should extend to personal ventures as well. Rather than trying to achieve your biggest goals all at once, learn to stage your dreams. In figuring which small steps to take, follow founders' practice of prioritizing experiments and feedback that are likely to separate success from failure. A startup might target experiments that will reveal whether there truly is a large enough customer base willing to pay for the company's planned product and what characteristics of the product would be most important to customers. Rather than trying to build out a full product, many startups create a minimum viable product with which to test the biggest of the uncertainties.[6]

For instance, instead of manufacturing his own shoes, Nike founder Phil Knight originally went to Onitsuka Tiger shoes in Japan to source and then distribute his products, enabling him to explore whether there was demand for a higher-quality running shoe before beginning to think about designing and making his own. Then, when cofounder Bill Bowerman used his wife's waffle iron to create the first sole with square spikes, Knight was poised to invest in developing it into the Waffle Trainer sneaker, which quickly became the top-selling training shoe in the United States.[7]

If your dream is to write a memoir, for example, but you're overwhelmed by the challenges of becoming a published writer, you can start by trying to post an essay or two about minor yet intriguing incidents in your life. Then, having gained experience and confidence, you can try a weightier piece about a big, pivotal incident. Monitor the reaction to that piece; strengthen your effort amid positive results, and adjust or abandon it amid negative ones. Once you've achieved smaller wins, you'll be much further along on the road to making the book a reality.

When I was founding chairman of the board of a new private boys' high school in Boston, our first-year math teacher was a Harvard-trained lawyer named Michael who had a love for math, had tutored high-school students in it, and thought he might want to teach the subject. He could have quit his job to become a math teacher, as did Kevin Compton, a partner at prominent venture capital firm Kleiner Perkins who caused waves in 2004 when he broke out of his powerful handcuffs to leave the firm and pursue his longtime passion to become a seventh-grade math teacher. However, to explore teaching, Michael decided to make a small leap instead. He kept his day job at the law firm but came to teach math for two days a week at the end of the day, from about 5:00 to 6:00 p.m. His first month of teaching highlighted for him the differences between tutoring and having to manage a full classroom of boys, and between being able to focus on a single student's needs and the needs of a class with widely varying capabilities. He completed his yearlong commitment and then returned to focusing full time on the law.

Other people who have an "I might want to teach" itch might explore opportunities to conduct a brown-bag lunch at their current employer or to teach a session in an adult-education program on a weekend. While working at L'Oréal as a product manager, Jordana believed deep down that she might want to find fulfillment in teaching and education. "So I 'dated' that field by spending my weekends teaching in a local community college here, volunteering in public schools during my free time, conducting workshops for college students when I could," she explained to me. "It was only after dating the field of teaching that that I felt confident enough to leave L'Oréal and work toward a career that will allow me to do something more related to education, something more personally fulfilling."

Staging can also help us avoid shocks and recriminations in our intimate relationships if big transitions go sour. Think back to Chapter 1 where we saw the consequences of Akhil's campaign to persuade Roopa that he should leap into a startup. Instead of selling a positive picture of the future in a quest to gain his fiancée's support—"*when* we raise capital from venture capitalists," "*when* we sell our first product to the Department of Defense"—Akhil should have expressed clearly the potential pitfalls in his plans and dreams and moved forward in stages so Roopa could fully appreciate and acclimate to the risks and opportunities. A message of "We might not raise capital by a year from now, and here is my plan for how we'll still be able to pay the bills if that happens. If the DoD doesn't sign on, we're also working on a medium-sized industrial customer that needs a cleantech solution" would have given Roopa the chance to gain greater confidence in Akhil's decision to become a founder. By staging his approach, Akhil would have been able to reverse decisions that looked too risky. Then both of them would have been better informed about the road ahead.

Motivate Change via Aspirations or Regret

Even when your head is telling you to change, your heart often fights any possible moves outside your comfort zone. The best entrepreneurs motivate themselves to get over this hurdle either with their focus on the prospects for a greater reward in the new venture or with their aversion to the pangs of regret.

Take Steve Jobs when trying to recruit his best friend, Steve Wozniak, to cofound what became Apple Computer. Wozniak, an engineer with a 200+ IQ and a penchant for extreme honesty, was at his dream job already, designing scientific calculators at computing pioneer Hewlett-Packard. In Wozniak's words, "I got to work on a product that at the time was the highlight product of the world. . . . I could never leave Hewlett-Packard. My plan . . . was to work at HP for life."[8] Not only was Jobs fighting against Wozniak's loyalty to HP, but he was also up against the advice of the person Wozniak looked up to most: Wozniak's father. "My dad had always told me that your job is the most important thing you'll ever have and the worst thing to lose."[9]

But, stage after stage, Jobs showed Wozniak the potential rewards of cofounding a personal-computer company. When Wozniak gave away copies of his schematics for the original Apple circuit boards, saying that he wanted the knowledge to be free to others, Jobs convinced him to start doing otherwise. To demonstrate that the team could make a profit, Jobs paid someone to draw up Wozniak's circuit boards, thinking that companies could buy the schematics for just under $15 each, even though Wozniak didn't believe the schematics would sell. Jobs appealed to Wozniak's sense of adventure, saying, "Even if we lose our money, we'll have a company."[10] Jobs sealed the deal by making his first sale. The first Apple customer didn't want the schematics that Wozniak had drawn up or to do any assembly: He wanted one hundred computers, fully built, and would pay about $500 apiece. The $50,000 order was more than twice Wozniak's annual salary. Jobs immediately called Wozniak at HP and said, "Are you sitting down?"[11] By showing Wozniak a real order for what had been a side hobby, Jobs was able to show his friend the potential of what they could build.

On the regret side, Jordana realized after leaving L'Oréal that she wanted to have a deeper, one-on-one impact on people, such as counseling people through difficult times in their lives, and that doing so would require her to get a clinical psychology degree on top of her MBA. She applied to graduate programs in psychology and was accepted by an excellent school. However, she immediately came under pressure from her parents to take a job in order to shed her student debt. "The psychology program will always be there," they argued adamantly, but her opportunities to take lucrative MBA jobs would disappear. As a result of these financial handcuffs, Jordana requested a deferral from the psychology program.

Over the next few weeks, the regret steadily built, and Jordana decided to pursue the psychology degree anyway. "What really gave me the courage to take the leap was that I knew in my heart that I would regret letting this opportunity pass. It has been a dream of mine to get that degree. As harsh as it sounds, I knew I'd hate myself if I didn't give this a go! I would be living with the knowledge that I once had the power and privilege to achieve a dream but chose not to. It would have a real psychological impact on my sense of self. This helped me gain the confidence to resist my parents." Even before starting her psychology program, Jordana was in tune with the fact that late in life, people harbor many more regrets over inaction than regrets over action.[12] Jordana's reflection on her potential regrets laid bare that she was substituting others' values for her own.

Time to Adjust Your Goal?

Say you have gone through painstaking preparation to test the first stage of your dream. But unlike Jordana, you figured out through that learning process that you shouldn't pursue that dream after all. Before walking away, ask yourself: Are there other versions of my idea that would be more practical? The answer is probably yes. It's easy to get locked into a dream's specifics. Try bending or replacing some of those specifics and see what you get. Maybe instead of starting an antibullying organization, you should aim to run an existing organization that already has a presence in elementary schools, or maybe you should aim to become the head of fundraising for such an organization. Those are still big, exciting dreams, but they might be more manageable.

I hope I've given you inspiration and a few useful tools to overcome your hesitations about starting out on a new road. At the same time I hope I haven't *over*energized you. As we've seen, an overabundance of passion for a venture, coupled with an underappreciation of the risks, can be just as sure a ticket to eventual regret as an inability to move forward, making it even more critical for you to temper your fervor.

TAKE CONTROL OF YOUR PASSION

A common cliché is that entrepreneurs jump out of planes and create their parachutes on the way down. In fact, the best founders do the opposite, fighting their impulse to leap into the unknown. As hard as it might be for the Akhils of the world to slow down and take a more head-driven approach to evaluating changes, the most effective entrepreneurs do so. The same is true when we find an area of life about which we are passionate and want to do the equivalent of making our favorite hobby into a full-time pursuit.

When the issue is pulling on reins, as opposed to breaking chains, we have to tap a different set of practices.

Focus on the Gray Areas

The best entrepreneurs check their impulses by creating some version of a Venn diagram of their circumstances and evaluating where they fall in three areas of readiness (see Figure 1). If they're not already in the center, they pause and work to proactively bring themselves out of a white or gray area into the black bullseye.

First, they ask whether the *market* is really willing to pay for their idea, rather than assuming that their passion for the idea will be echoed by many other people. Texas executive Barry Nalls had worked for the large telecommunications company GTE for a decade when he decided to become a founder: "I had a desire to start a company with all of the functional knowledge I had gotten from GTE. I was looking to own my own company." However, his first attempt failed because there was little demand for the services he wanted to offer. "There were two absolutely painful parts: that I never got a day off and that this was all my money. With the money, when there's no payroll, it means you have no money either. So you're as broke as you can get. It was very tough financially and emotionally," he said. He returned to GTE and learned how to test the market to tell whether there was sufficient demand to build a sustain-

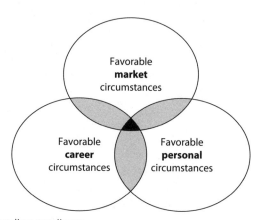

FIGURE 1. Founding readiness

able business and how to roll out the product if the market demand was there. After another decade at GTE, he left again and founded the very successful telecommunications startup Masergy. Now his planning "was very similar to building a business plan for a product roll-out at GTE." He asked himself a series of questions: "What do I know? I know telecom, so the business should be in that. Who do I know? Enterprise clients. What do these enterprise clients care about when it comes to telecom? What are they willing to pay for?"[13]

Second, entrepreneurs ask whether they've developed the *career* skills and resources, including networks, to make the new initiative happen. After the failure of his first startup, Nalls realized that he was missing knowledge of how to develop and deploy new products and that he did not have any contacts among small companies. He aggressively filled those holes by taking control of his career path within GTE—for example, changing positions there every eighteen to twenty-four months to diversify his product experience and make his network more robust.

Third, they ask whether their *personal* situations are ready and supportive. Can their families accommodate the leap? Nalls, who had lived in Texas all his life, relocated his family to Los Angeles when he started Masergy, but he soon realized that the L.A. schools could not meet the needs of his son, who had autism. Acting quickly to recover, Nalls moved his family back to Texas and commuted every other week to L.A. He made his bimodal solution work, but it slowed down the venture a little. As he explained to me, proactive assessment of what could go wrong for his family—"What if our son's assigned speech therapist isn't experienced with autism? Will L.A.'s higher cost of living prevent us from paying out of pocket for a new therapist?"—would have enabled him to create a smoother path for his wife and son (and himself).[14]

You can use this Venn diagram approach any time you're envisioning a major change. If you're eager to switch careers, for example, see whether your circumstances really do support your new path. Scrutinize any unfavorable circumstances, look at whether you're in a gray area, and work on getting closer to the bullseye. You'll have to modify the diagram a bit, of course: Unless you're planning to launch a business, you'll want to change "market" to something more relevant, such as the size and value of the opportunity you might pursue. Will it be exciting? Growth enhancing? Lucrative?

Other questions to ask yourself include: Which of the three factors is most important and thus deserves to be bigger than the others in the diagram? What is your threshold of favorability, or the number of factors that have to be favorable for you to make a change? Do you need to be in the bullseye by having all three factors fully favorable, or are you willing to leap if you're in a gray area? Most important if you're doing this proactively, how can you use the analysis to improve the favorability of any factors that fall short?

Two of my executive MBA students used the Venn diagram approach to evaluate decisions they were inclined to green-light: whether they and their spouses should try to have another child. For one of the students, this would be his second child; for the other, his third. From the beginning, I had been impressed with how family oriented these students were, and they were explicit about really enjoying quality time with their young children. In each student's analysis, his three circles related to his spouse's stage of career, their ability to support the family financially, and his stage of career. Their three factors didn't have equal importance and thus didn't deserve to be the same sizes on their diagram. In particular, they both prioritized their spouses' stage of career and made it the largest of the three circles, though they differed in their sizing of the other two circles and their evaluation of the current favorability of each factor.

The most interesting part of their discussion focused on their threshold of favorability: Would they need to be in the bullseye, with all three factors favorable, or might they move ahead even if one factor was missing? They surprised themselves by deciding that the spouse factor and at least one and a half of the others would have to be favorable—a fairly high standard that they realized they weren't able to meet. They were not at their threshold of favorability. Their wives were at iffy career stages, they needed to shore up their savings, and they were making changes in their own job trajectories.

One student came up with a concrete plan that he thought could get his family to two and a half favorable factors within a couple of years, though: "Right now, my child is in day care that we have to pay for, but when he's in a public school, the financial burden will be reduced, and we can reevaluate. Also right now, I have to travel a lot for work even though I want to be present for my kids. Maybe I can build up my team to the point where they can do more of the heavy lifting and can do the traveling for me so I won't have to do it." Those actions, shown in Figure 2, would move him closer to the bullseye and get him to his two-and-a-half threshold.

Clear-headed evaluation of career opportunities can also spark productive conversations. Andrew and Diane, a married couple in their early thirties, were employed as senior managers within their family's business in Ohio. They enjoyed their professional autonomy, influence within the company, stable

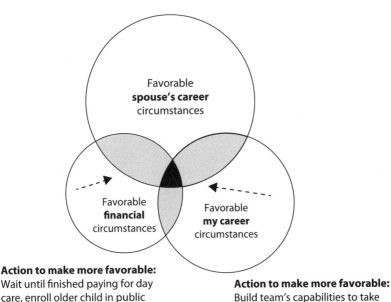

Action to make more favorable:
Wait until finished paying for day
care, enroll older child in public
school

Action to make more favorable:
Build team's capabilities to take
on more travel responsibilities

FIGURE 2. Readiness to have another child
Note: Sizes of circles reflect relative importance.

income, and work-life balance. They were also expecting their first child and
eagerly anticipating tapping nearby relatives for babysitting assistance.

However, Andrew had long nursed a dream of working at an exciting,
high-pressure Silicon Valley tech startup. A few casual early conversations with
a high-profile Silicon Valley–based startup had turned into a compelling job
offer. In many ways, the job was everything Andrew had ever dreamed of. First,
it brought him back to the technology sector, a space that he had greatly enjoyed working in for several years after graduating from college but then left to
oversee his family's business. Succeeding in a hands-on role within the family
business had brought him operational credibility, which in turn meant more
interesting—and highly selective—career opportunities going forward. From
a Venn diagram perspective, Andrew's first two circles were tech sector and
startup opportunity. On these they were a rousing two for two!

Andrew and Diane knew that compelling job offers were few and far between. Yet the job could destroy the work-life balance they currently enjoyed,
just as a child was on the way. Worse still, moving to San Francisco entailed
leaving the family support—and free childcare—they expected to tap. Andrew

told my research assistant: "Everyone in my family leveraged our network of aunts, uncles, cousins, and grandparents. Our family is so big that no one has ever even sent a kid to day care before. It was just that easy to drop your kid off at a relative's house. If we moved to San Francisco, the responsibility of raising the baby would primarily fall to Diane, given the eighty-plus hours per week I'd be working. We could hire a nanny, but that decision didn't sit well with us. We also weren't ready to send an infant to day care." Andrew's parents were also adamantly against the move. "To my parents, the thought of us moving to San Francisco right before the birth of their first grandchild was devastating. They told us that we had no idea what kind of support a child needed and that leaving to take a high-pressure job right when a kid was on the way was the definition of insanity."

These considerations added their third circle, family support. After a frank discussion, it was clear to both of them that the circumstances they faced were far from favorable. Ultimately, the couple decided to forfeit the job in San Francisco. "The timing just wasn't right. I'm hoping that, after we have another child and they're both a little older, I'll be able to revisit this opportunity or one like it." With the lessons learned and with time to plan, they could proactively find solutions to many of the challenges—and handcuffs, both financial and psychic—that had ended pursuit of Andrew's opportunity but would not necessarily torpedo a future one.

Perfect Your Pitch by Taking a "Pillars" Approach

Once you've identified the gray areas that prevent you from having circumstances that are as favorable as possible, consider what variables need to change in order to hit the mark. Research by Geoff Smart, founder of the G. H. Smart startup-hiring consultancy, shows that job seekers can maximize their chances of success by thinking through what he refers to as the three pillars of career switching. As Smart explained to me, "In strategizing around your own career success, it's really important not to change too many variables at once." The three pillars can be summarized by the following three questions: What type of customer do you target in your present job—are you selling to consumers, businesses, governments, or even a board or committee? What type of product—such as consumer goods, enterprise software, marketing services, or your unique insights—are you selling to that customer? Finally, what's the main challenge you face on a day-to-day basis?

For career switchers, Smart advises changing one pillar per job switch. Leaving all the pillars unchanged may be a recipe for stagnation; changing too many may be a recipe for excessive risk.

> Say that there's someone who is very successful at selling software services to human resources divisions within Fortune 500 companies. Then, that person changes one thing in their repertoire—let's say product. The individual now starts selling payroll services to HR divisions at Fortune 500 companies. You could still see how that person would be successful. But if you had somebody who was selling a completely different product to a completely different customer in a completely different industry, they don't have a lot of past strength to call on. They don't have a lot of networks to call upon for help. It's pretty difficult to have folks succeeding where two or three pillars are new.

To practice Smart's approach, think ahead to an interview you might have with a potential employer. When you're changing one pillar, you can often make a compelling pitch for why you'll bring a great mix of excitement for your new pillar combined with a foundation of experience that you'll leverage from your other two pillars. If you're changing more than one pillar, practice your pitch and see whether your argument would still be compelling for a potential hirer. Ask individuals who have already landed your dream role what skill sets underpin their success at work. To find the weakest parts of your pitch, identify which gaps in your experience an interviewer would prioritize as problems. What proactive steps can you take to fill these holes? For instance, if you work in business-to-business sales but have your eye on business-to-consumer opportunities, can you ask your current employer if you can spend a few hours a week helping the part of the business that sells to consumers? Use this pitching litmus test to both identify upcoming challenges and develop ways to address them ahead of time.

I tell potential applicants to our MBA program to use the same litmus test: Try to fill out the MBA application with your best "pitch" for why you should be admitted, see if there are parts of that pitch that are still weak, and try to proactively shore up those parts. By doing so, you're forcing yourself to look through the eyes of a potential hirer or admissions committee. A key issue for applicants may be that they don't know—or worse still, incorrectly guess—what a selective program wants from its incoming class. To address this problem, make the best use of your own insider network, asking a few key individuals who know the program intimately to review your application and highlight its weaknesses. After consulting an experienced MBA graduate, one "quant"—a student with a financial, math, or engineering background—who found that she had trouble vividly conveying her leadership experiences in the application waited one more year in order to enrich her work experience (leading a project team for several months) and took on a leadership role in a communal activity. To ease doubts in another direction, a "poet"—a student with a liberal arts background who realized that the admissions committee might question his quantitative ability—took the advice of an advisor to enroll in a demanding corporate-finance course and got an A. (This process might also help the candidate consider whether to even pursue an MBA to begin with.) With the luxury of time and a measure of forethought, you can strengthen your qualifications and your pitch.

Entrepreneurs face the same three-pillars challenges. Serial entrepreneurs who in their next startups changed multiple variables—the industry, the location, or the macroeconomic conditions (because they waited longer than average before getting back on the horse)—performed worse than counterparts who made fewer changes.[15] The founder of the restaurant chain Noodles and Company encountered the pillars problem when a newly hired CEO turned out to be a mismatch for the job. The move entailed too many changes for the executive: from one industry subsegment to another and from a big, corporate milieu that was quite steady to a fast-moving, aggressive culture. Conscious of changing too many dimensions at once, the founder next tapped someone with a better mix of pillar changes versus continuity.

To be sure, we can all come up with people who changed multiple pillars and still thrived. It's important for us to have such role models to motivate us through difficult times, and we love seeing people make dramatic changes in their lives and still come out ahead. However, we can't let our striving to become like them—and the fact they are rare outliers rather than the norm—lead us to make ill-conceived decisions at key turning points in our lives. There is a direct parallel to budding entrepreneurs who can all come up with first-time founders who led their companies to industry-dominating status and remained in control throughout. However, when I ask founders to name those role models, the same names (Bill Gates, Steve Jobs, Mark Zuckerberg!) always recur, highlighting their rarity. Further highlighting their rarity, my students dive enthusiastically into my challenge to list ten such founders, eager to prove me wrong. When I take a show of hands, the students fall far short of ten.

Moreover, many of those they do name do not belong on the list. For example, Bill Gates and Steve Jobs are always among the first names thrown out. However, for Gates, Microsoft wasn't the first startup he founded with Paul Allen. For his part, Jobs was never in control of Apple as CEO for its first two decades of life; it wasn't until the company was a phoenix rising from the ashes that Jobs became CEO. Often lauded as key exemplars, Gates and Jobs are actually misleading role models.

Continuing to develop, innovate, and stretch by a pillar can be refreshing and challenging, while you make sure that your passion for a change doesn't lead to counterproductive overstretching.

Try Before You Buy

When I was finally looking to leave Harvard Business School, we wanted to relocate to a city where we had family, after having no relatives in the Boston area for so long. It was tempting to pursue the first attractive opportunity that came along: a new, high-profile engineering school that wanted to build its entrepreneurship program and was located near two of our children. However, I decided to take incremental steps to "date" potential opportunities, keeping my position at Harvard but being a visiting professor at other schools. From those visits, I was able to see how the institutions differed, reflect on my prioritization of those differences, and experience each of them from the inside before having to decide which one to adopt as my next long-term home. In contrast to the approach of taking small, targeted leaps that we discussed above, wherein you focus on specific uncertainties but not on the full range of issues, these visits enabled me to live as if I had made a full leap, experiencing most of the job as if I had already moved to the new school. A mistaken visit could be far more easily undone, though, than a mistaken job change.

I was taking a page from successful entrepreneurs, many of whom try out new ventures before committing themselves fully. Compared with people who jump directly from being employees into being full-time founders, entrepreneurs who launch ventures on the side while keeping their existing jobs are 33 percent less likely to fail in their startups because they use a staged approach to learning about the new business.[16] Of the founders attending my workshops over the years, 26 percent initially worked part time on the startup while keeping their day jobs (and salaries).

Just as staging can help break handcuffs, trying before you buy can help control your passion. Craft small experiments in a low-pressure environment to test if you like the new career, or new employer, as much as you imagine. Not everyone can easily structure introductory part-time roles with a prospective employer, but you can try to find creative short-term arrangements that accomplish the same goal. In other words, "date" before you "marry"; once you are married to a job, it will become much harder to reverse your commitments. If things aren't as rosy as you had imagined, your decision is easy to undo, as you didn't give up your existing position. Better still, you may have learned how to shave down your commitments at work or figured out a way to juggle your incremental responsibilities at work and home, making your next "test project" that much easier to pick up.

People who want to contribute to a social enterprise but aren't sure if their for-profit skills will be useful in that new arena can try volunteering at a nonprofit by spearheading a well-defined project for the organization. In my experience, two areas where nonprofits can benefit from for-profit expertise are governance practices and financial processes. Chat with a member of the nonprofit's board of directors about how they enforce accountability. Do they conduct regular reviews and evaluations of the organization's CEO, or could they use help with instituting such a process and developing an evaluation form? Even rarer, does the board conduct regular reviews of itself to find ways to improve? If you find a for-profit practice from which the nonprofit can benefit, collaborate with that board member on a part-time project to introduce that practice. With financial processes, if a chat with the organization's head of finance highlights a budgeting best practice that might help and she is open to adopting it, work on a project to incorporate it into their existing processes.

These projects will enable you to see if your hoped-for impact can become reality or whether the organization is resistant to your ideas, and thus whether you should deepen the relationship. Try them out on a part-time basis that is easily reversed because you kept your day job, but in the process see if you want to commit fully while giving them a chance to see if they want to commit to you.

Needless to say, these lessons can be extended to actual dating, where uninformed passion can be misleading and dating—done right—can yield big benefits. Amid your early passion for the person, use dating to surface issues that could become problematic if discovered much further down the line, or that could enhance your relationship if discovered now. If religion is important to you, delve into his faith and religious practices and evaluate whether they are compatible with your own. Explore what type of relationship you each aspire to have: one that might culminate in marriage with children, a marriage in which children aren't part of the equation, or a relationship in which marriage is never mentioned. Is she a saver, as you are, or a spender who likes living beyond her means? Would she pooh-pooh your distress when your joint checking account dipped below $5,000? Assessing this is akin to potential cofounders who evaluate whether one cofounder wants to spend a lot of money on early tests of the idea or on marketing while the other wants to conserve cash. Anticipate the deal breakers that could be devastating if they were discovered months or years from now (or after marriage) and find ways while you are dating to front-load your learning about whether they exist.

The dark side of trying before buying is the risk of being overwhelmed by possibilities. Zero choice may bring unhappiness, but unhappiness also escalates as we go from having few choices to many.[17] In the 1960s, Joe Coulombe's Los Angeles–based Pronto Markets were having trouble competing with the wide selections at other stores. In 1967, he founded the Trader Joe's grocery chain. One of its foundational concepts was to limit product selection: Trader Joe's stocks three thousand to four thousand items per store, a fraction of the offerings at competing stores, which might stock as many as fifty thousand items.[18] As a result its sales per square foot are the highest in the industry and twice that of direct competitor Whole Foods, which stocks more than twenty thousand items in a typical store.[19] Job hunters can also become unhappy with too many choices. Barry Schwartz, a professor of psychology at Swarthmore College and author of *The Paradox of Choice*, studied 548 job-seeking college seniors at eleven schools from October through their graduation in June. Students who relentlessly evaluated every last option—"maximizers"—landed jobs with 20 percent higher salary on average, but they felt worse about the outcome. "The maximizer is kicking himself because he can't examine every option and at some point had to just pick something," Schwartz says.[20] Schwartz recommends that maximizers lower their sights and just select a choice that meets predetermined core requirements. Then they can focus on the positive attributes of that choice and let go of the other options.

Another caution: Don't overestimate how much "dating" approximates "marriage." Even after experiencing a new activity in a small dose, we still have to watch for ways in which that experience may be different from the one we would have if we were to dive in fully. For my kids, visiting California is not a true taste of what it would be like to live there. When I was a visiting professor, I had to remind myself not to overextrapolate from that experience to the one I would have as a full-time faculty member at the same school. This is even true for literal dating and marriage. Despite the romantic expectations of how living together would help unmarried couples figure out whether marriage should be in their future, a Penn State team led by family scholar Claire Kamp Dush found that among 1,425 US couples, those who had lived together reported significantly poorer marital quality and experienced significantly higher marital instability than those who had not lived together.[21] Enter into your dating with eyes wide open, not just about your potential mate but also about how well the situation approximates the full situation you eventually hope to face.

Get Outside Eyes That Aren't Looking Through Your Rose-Colored Lenses

Even when we think our own eyes are wide open, we're often misled by our passion. Neuroscientist Tali Sharot cautions that we are wired to wear rose-colored glasses, whether we are underestimating the probability of getting divorced or overestimating our chances of success on the job market.[22] (Recall the small-business owners who severely overestimated their startup's prospects?) To be realistic, you'll almost certainly need some intellectual distance to counteract your heart's desire to leap forward. If it's a career move, do some due diligence on the new position to avoid a "grass is greener elsewhere" bias. Maybe borrow the Take Your Daughter to Work Day concept by tagging along with someone who works in the field you're considering (even if the person doesn't look old enough to have birthed you).

If you can't counteract these emotions yourself, lean on other people. Airbnb was founded in late 2007 by Brian Chesky, Joe Gebbia, and Nathan Blecharczyk. The company's first advisors came from the Y Combinator accelerator program, including such startup luminaries as Y Combinator founder Paul Graham. Graham stepped in with key advice during the earliest days of Airbnb, when most potential users hadn't heard of the company and the few who had weren't using its service. The team had tried everything they knew to get users excited about their platform, but "nothing was working," said Gebbia. "Graham . . . got us out of our comfort zone, and [made us] talk to people using our service in New York."[23] Though Graham didn't know exactly how to solve the problem, he did know that speaking to users would likely uncover the source of the issue. In New York, the founders booked rooms with Airbnb hosts, stayed in their homes, and chatted with them about the service. In doing so, they learned that the unflattering, grainy photographs of homes listed on the site led to many would-be renters sticking with more familiar hotel options.

So Airbnb hired photographers to capture room layouts; rentals spiked. Graham's advice enabled the founders to home in on a key issue within a few weeks rather than months or even years.

Recognizing the value that outside advisors can bring, many of the best entrepreneurs assemble a personal board of advisors or tap into a formal CEO's forum to give them a dose of realism. We can do likewise by systematically identifying and approaching advisors to help us think through challenges we're facing. Chesky himself, now CEO of Airbnb, goes straight to the source, identifying the single best authority on a topic and then asking for help. As Airbnb scaled in size, Chesky was able to tap knowledge—usually just by asking for a meeting or call—from other founders, including Facebook's Mark Zuckerberg and Amazon's Jeff Bezos. (My own experiences reinforce this impression: Founders are usually extremely generous in giving back to the next generation of entrepreneurs, even flying cross-country at their own expense to participate in a section of my course for eighty minutes.) In addition to tapping thought leaders in similar fields, Chesky would also synthesize divergent ideas by going to unexpected or tangential sources for insight. For example, when faced with a hiring dilemma, instead of seeking out the head of a large company's HR division, he might go to a Hollywood movie agent whose career depends on attracting talent. Chesky is constantly building his network of advisors. From Jony Ive, Apple's head of design, he learned that Apple can fit all of its products onto one kitchen table—underscoring the company's emphasis on focus. Leaning on well-versed outsiders has helped Chesky fill the gaps in his own knowledge as Airbnb scaled.[24]

How can you make it compelling for those outside eyes to spend time helping you? Great founders do small projects or favors for major influencers as a way of establishing goodwill and building strong networks. Phil Knight became close to his coach, the legendary Bill Bowerman, who later created the first Nike shoe sole, the waffle pattern, using—indeed—his kitchen's waffle iron.[25] Knight served as Bowerman's guinea pig by becoming the first runner in a competition to use a shoe custom-designed by Bowerman.[26] By doing so, Knight solidified the relationship he needed to eventually convert Bowerman into a partner at Blue Ribbon Sports, the precursor to Nike.

Cultivating relationships like these can give you insight into challenges you'll face in your new endeavor as well as the potential compensating benefits likely to come from making a bold move. Talk to people who have made the decision to move forward with plans similar to yours or have substantial experience in what you're doing—not just friends who are a year or two ahead of you at similar jobs or people whose personal relationship with you precludes their giving you frank criticism. If you're to understand the key challenges, you need someone who is experienced as well as frank—and willing to ask you the hard questions, much as an actual board of directors has to do. An advisor like that can assist you in learning more cheaply the lessons for which others have had to pay a stiff tuition bill. They can also help you work out ways to handle or even mitigate problems ahead of time.

These advisors can help you resist the temptation to sell your significant other a rosy picture of the path ahead. A valued advisor could have pushed Akhil to proactively approach Roopa and talk frankly about his ambitions to start a business and what that would likely mean for their family, both the good and the bad. The advisor could have suggested that Akhil probe his fiancée's fears and brainstorm about how to address them, either through better preparation or by adjusting the timing of his leap. The sooner someone like Akhil addresses these dynamics, the more effectively he'll be able to manage them.

This approach also applies to issues we face in our personal lives. Say your toddler has been diagnosed with a learning disability you are confident you can handle. Still, finding another family whose adolescent child received a similar diagnosis will help you ensure that you truly understand the longer-term implications and how to get your child the support he needs. Think back to how Barry Nalls was blindsided by the L.A. school system's deficiencies in special-needs services. Proactively finding and talking to L.A. families with children who had autism could have saved him two costly and wrenching moves. Although it's impossible to forecast every eventuality, focusing on common major problems—or issues that are particularly costly to you—can unearth potential hazards.

But Stay Excited!

Sometimes when I talk to students or would-be entrepreneurs about strategies for managing risk, they accuse me (only half-jokingly) of trying to extinguish their passion. How can they stay excited about a life change, they ask, if they have to sketch Venn diagrams, think about pillars, and get outside eyes?

When I hear this, I ask whether they're aware that the origin of the word *passion* is a Latin root that means "to suffer." I don't want to diminish their excitement; I do want to help them minimize the suffering that is too often an element of passion.

In trying to mitigate suffering, I hope I don't convey the impression that I believe in trying to drain the emotion from major life moves. Quite the opposite! I fully appreciate the positive role of emotion in making choices. Even if founders could completely sideline their emotions, the result would be worse decisions, and the same is true for our nonfounding decisions. For instance, the neuroscientist Anthony Damasio writes of a patient whose frontal brain surgery left him essentially undamaged except for a loss of emotions—the patient felt neither pleasure nor anguish. This doesn't sound so bad—there are probably times in all of our lives when we wish we could get off the roller coaster of emotions. But in fact it was a catastrophic deficiency. Despite being sound of mind in every other way, the patient was unable to make sensible, well-thought-out decisions. His ventures ended in bankruptcy. He lost his savings. He divorced his wife, remarried, and divorced again. He was unable to learn from his mistakes. This patient and a series of others with similar deficits led Damasio to conclude that emotions play a crucial role in supporting decisions.[27]

Emotion is organic to our existence—we can never eliminate it from our endeavors; nor should we try. The challenge, as we see in the next chapter, is harnessing it: getting it to work *with* us instead of against us so that we can achieve a productive balance of head and heart. This applies both to the challenging depths of failure and to the exciting heights of success.

CHAPTER 3

WILL FAILURE—AND SUCCESS—
BRING YOU DOWN?

WE ALL CARRY MENTAL PICTURES of ourselves in new roles we would really enjoy. Harnessed constructively, these images can have a powerful motivational effect. However, many of us also carry around highly demotivating images of what might happen if we tried to pursue our dreams and fell short. We become hesitant because the path forward would require us to learn unfamiliar skills, leave our support networks, and risk our reputations, all on the bet that a better future might result. If you were one of the many kids who took piano lessons, think about the pride you felt when you had perfected a piece and wanted to show it off to everyone. Now compare that to a week later when you were struggling to conquer a brand-new tune and didn't want any of your family, let alone the neighbors, to hear.

In our most vulnerable moments, we might even envision extreme consequences of failure: We end up jobless, short of cash, without assets, dependent on others, alone, unappreciated, humiliated—and on and on in a Dickensian tragedy. That fear of failure is a powerful force preventing us from exploring the limits of our potential.

On the flip side, when we indulge in imagining what success would look like, we tend not to give much thought to its potential consequences. How will the demands on me change if I get that promotion I really want? What if my girlfriend actually does say yes to my proposal and we have to plan a wedding on our tight budget? What if my oldest child gets into the prestigious school I might not be able to afford?

In other words, we're not very good at thinking constructively about either failure or success. In that respect, we can learn a great deal from entrepreneurs.

Founders quickly become acquainted with failure; the great ones also experience success—often interspersed with the failures. They come to know the taste, smell, and texture of big losses and spectacular wins. This familiarity breeds a set of unusual approaches to both. As we'll see, founders practice antifragility, to borrow terminology from Nassim Nicholas Taleb, and draw strength from losses.[1] They set up safeguards to protect themselves, become more comfortable with the idea of failure, and learn how to fail productively. While keeping the threat of failure in mind, they lay the groundwork for the potentially challenging consequences of success—in case their dreams really do come true.

FEAR OF FAILURE CAN UNDERMINE YOU

Take, as an example, Lauren Kay, who founded and became CEO of the Dating Ring, a high-potential startup adding a touch of offline personal matchmaking to the otherwise impersonal online search for companionship. Cofounder Emma Tessler, a self-described "relationship and sexuality specialist" (she had been a sex-ed teacher in Harlem), would be chief happiness officer. They began honing their plans, started developing their site and matchmaking model, and headed out to search for funding.

Early on, they decided to be one of thousands of startups competing for a scarce slot in the prestigious Y Combinator startup incubator. YC, as it is known, has helped birth industry-changing startups like Dropbox, Air, Stripe, Reddit, and Zenefits. Kay and Tessler won the lottery. They were admitted to YC's January 2014 class; meanwhile, 98 percent of their fellow applicants had been turned away.

Kay described the messages that were drilled into them during their three months at YC: "You've made it into an extremely exclusive club of startup founders. . . . Your job in the startup world is to run these hypergrowth companies that are so magical that people are willing to pump tens of millions of dollars into them, sometimes raising billions of dollars. You're defining this new future." They were building a revolutionary company that would challenge the status quo. To do that, they would have to get big fast. If one of the YC startups were to decide that it wanted more modest growth, Kay said that the reaction would be, "Why are you here? Why are you at YC? You're not cut out for the big leagues. . . . It's like being at the Olympics and people are talking about doing well in their club-sports league."[2]

Coming out of YC, Kay and Tessler were riding high, getting lots of attention from potential investors and growing 10 percent each week. In addition to their initial $100,000 investment from YC, they raised $255,000 from angel investors, affluent people who were investing their own money. In April 2015, they were featured in a *New York Times* article, "Start-Up Blends Old-Fashioned Matchmaking and Algorithms."[3]

However, things quickly became a lot tougher. They began experiencing flat revenues and a lack of growth in their user base. After persevering through several tough stretches, they began questioning their futures. During one of their difficult moments, an interviewer asked, "What are you afraid is going to happen?" After thinking a bit, Kay answered very soberly that she was "afraid of running out of money, and then I'll have to leave the company, and I'll be a miserable failure." The company had been a very public endeavor, and if it were to shut down, everyone would know. Kay would have to go back to an old employer. "It definitely would be swallowing my pride to be back to where I was before."[4]

Kay's parents had also invested tens of thousands of dollars in the Dating Ring. To Kay, shutting down the company would feel like she had broken a promise to her mother. "I was used to doing what I had told them I would do. I felt like I had failed and it made me most embarrassed when it came to my parents. It seemed like I would be admitting to them this huge failure that they didn't see coming."[5]

Her cofounder, Tessler, was even more emotional about such a scenario: "Everyone is going to know that I'm a failure, that I said I could do it my way. I knew it was nontraditional, and I asked everyone to have faith in me, but I would prove all of them right—the ones who said that I'm going to fail."[6]

Fearing the prospect of public failure, Kay and Tessler wrestled with whether to continue pursuing the YC mantra of hypergrowth, and thus bear the increasing risk of failing completely, or to scale back their ambitions and try to build a smaller company. On the heels of voicing their fears of failure, they decided to cancel an imminent meeting with a potential investor and dramatically scale back their growth plans. Kay left the startup, decided within days to apply to graduate school, and then realized that she was doing so only "to have a clear cut answer to the dark and stormy 'What Are You Doing With

Your Life' cloud." Instead, she decided to push the pause button, saying, "Hopping from one job to the next is like breaking up with your partner only once you've lined up a new one. You're likely to repeat all of the same mistakes, because you haven't yet had a chance to reflect."[7] She tutored people part time, ran, and cooked, while interviewing for full-time jobs, none of which appealed to her. Kay admitted, "I was confused about who I was and what I was doing."[8]

This "What do I do next?" phase lasted for a year, until a meeting with Tessler. Her former cofounder asked, "You're happy with this life—why do anything else?" Kay realized, "I *was* happy, except that other people thought I should be doing more." Soon after, Tessler herself left the Dating Ring as it scaled back to a smaller company, was taken over by one of their long-time matchmakers, and became a profitable small business. Tessler went back to school to finish college with the goal of getting a master's degree and becoming a therapist. She looked back at the pressure-packed days of the Dating Ring with mixed emotions: "A lot of my identity was running the company, and not having that is a loss. . . . [But now] the idea of running a business makes me want to jump off a bridge."[9]

Despite the image we might have of the fearless entrepreneur, Kay and Tessler are far from alone in having their fear of failure drive important decisions. The Global Entrepreneurship Monitor (GEM) project studies entrepreneurial perceptions in dozens of countries, estimating such things as the percentage of people who perceive the presence of entrepreneurial opportunities in their countries, whether they are confident that they have the capability to start a business, and whether entrepreneurship is a good career choice. GEM also reports data on how common it is that the fear of failure would foreclose important career options for people. The result is pretty consistent: whether the countries are factor-driven economies (e.g., Algeria, Venezuela), efficiency-driven economies (e.g., Argentina, Hungary, Russia), or innovation-driven economies (e.g., Finland, Singapore, United States), 30–40 percent of the people say that fear of failure would prevent them from even starting to set up a business.[10]

The fear of failure is probably even more common among nonentrepreneurs than among entrepreneurs. Reflecting on more than a decade of experience as a therapist, Tellman Knudson says, "Ask the average person why they haven't accomplished their goals yet, and fear of failure will always crop up as the #1 block to success for most people, most of the time."[11]

These goals can be deeply personal. Writer Steph Compton had some powerful reflections about a long-time friend, about whom she says, "No one has ever known me as well as [he did]." He was one of her oldest and closest friends, someone with whom she could be herself without hiding anything and could "talk to for hours on end without ever running out of conversation." She longed to ask him about deepening their relationship and becoming significant others. However, she hesitated—if he didn't feel the same way, would it hurt the friendship? After weeks of delay, she finally got up the courage to "come clean, lay it all on the line." That day, she found out that he had just started dating another woman. The irony: She had hesitated because she didn't want to ruin the friendship. "Turns out, a new girlfriend can have a very similar effect," she wryly observed. Her hesitation to risk a friendship sparked real regrets about not reaching for a more meaningful relationship: "If time travel was a real thing, I would go back to myself a few months ago and punch myself in the face. . . . Life wouldn't be life without some regrets; some are acceptable, entertaining even, but some will haunt you. This one is the latter."[12]

All it takes is a few haunting hesitations like that to make us hypercautious. Most of us are familiar with the hypercautious mind-set. It's what causes you to vigilantly observe every step you take for days after you've sprained your ankle stepping off a curb. But the prevent-more-losses attitude can also get you into trouble. In cautiously monitoring your steps, you fail to watch for oncoming traffic as you cross the street or change your gait in ways that overtax other muscles and put your other ankle at risk.

Behind this impulse is a natural and well-documented human bias: the tendency toward loss aversion. We tend to strongly prefer avoiding losses over making gains.[13] A little conservatism by itself may not be a problem, but it fundamentally colors how we view losses. In fact, our instinct to avoid failure keeps us from fully acknowledging failure when it does happen. This makes it hard for us to make the most of our difficulties and, ideally, turn them into opportunities. We fear failure so much that we end up making situations worse: We get defensive and try to blame others when we should be cooperating to stanch the losses and regain momentum.

The avoid-losses mind-set can come to haunt us in a larger sense as we make our way through middle age. Often, the big initiatives that might have given us intense satisfaction get pushed aside by a thousand small responsibilities, many of which are primarily aimed at such things as pleasing our bosses and mollifying our detractors: updating numbers in a report that barely changes month to month, preparing yet another slide deck on a dead-end project, writing an exhaustive response to a colleague's sniping. We end up asking ourselves, "Where are the bold actions, the extraordinary initiatives?"

Fearing small failures, we create big regrets.

Pause for Reflection

For now, consider:

- Do you hesitate to seize intriguing opportunities for fear of not succeeding at them?

- Much like the young piano player who avoids practicing a new piece in front of others, do you avoid situations in which you will have to do something new in public?

- If you think about the worst situation you might face if you had failed, how hard would it have been, really, to recover from that failure?

- If your worries have prevented you from pursuing a goal, do you have any regrets now about not pursuing it?

SOMETIMES WE FAIL TO PLAN FOR SUCCESS

The same questions can help you address an alternative—but related—problem: thinking through and planning for the ramifications of *reaching* our goals. As Winston Churchill said, "The problems of victory are more agreeable than those of defeat, but they are no less difficult."[14] If it seems that I'm talking about an unlikely luxury, consider some of the very real consequences of the failure to prepare.

Success introduces problems. For instance, about 26 percent of students who are admitted to their first-choice college are unable to attend those schools because they can't afford them.[15] A similar picture arises for homeowners who achieve their dream of owning a house. For instance, in 2011, in the aftermath of a recession, 12.1 million US households were underwater on their mortgages, and even after years of recovery, millions were still in the same position in 2017.[16]

In the world of work, the Peter Principle conceptualizes the common but unexpected phenomenon of promoting people past the level of their competence.[17] Employees who perform well at one level often fall short at the next because they fail to meet the demands of the new position and then can't move up from there. This concept applies when the star salesperson is promoted to sales manager, or when a top researcher is named the head of an academic department.

Given the fast rate with which startups pass through stages, and the subsequently increasing and differing demands at each stage, founders can epitomize the Peter Principle. Take the example of Hamdi Ulukaya, founder of the Greek yogurt company Chobani. Ulukaya grew up in a small village in Turkey, the son of Kurdish farmers who made cheese and yogurt. In the middle of studying political science at Ankara University, he left Turkey in 1994 because of the government's oppression of its Kurdish minority group and came to the United States to study English and then to take business courses.[18] He decided that American yogurt left something to be desired. "I found American yogurt to be disgusting—too sugary and watery. If I wanted yogurt, I usually made it myself at home. So in 2005, when I came across a piece of junk mail advertising a yogurt factory for sale by Kraft, who was exiting the business, I was curious."[19] He bought the factory.

Within three years, Chobani had grabbed the number-one market share in the enormous yogurt industry. In Ulukaya's words, "Within a couple of weeks after Chobani got into ShopRite, we started getting orders for 5,000 cases. The first time we received one, I kept double-checking to make sure it didn't say 500. It quickly became clear that our biggest challenge wasn't going to be selling enough yogurt—it was going to be making enough yogurt." He was right: By 2014, sales had passed $1 billion. He was a smashing success and was now fielding calls from investors who were interested in financing Chobani's shocking growth. "Greek yogurt was becoming so popular that bigger players such as Dannon and Yoplait were going to launch their own. We needed to grow quickly enough to prevent established companies from stealing the market we'd created. For a while I took calls and meetings with private equity firms. They try to make you doubt yourself—it's a standard part of their pitch. I kept hearing the same things over and over: 'You've never done this before.' 'This is not a world for a start-up.'"[20]

In the face of this negative feedback, he became more confident. Reasoning with himself, he recognized that most of his early decisions had been right, so why was expansion going to be any different? "Besides money, what could these guys bring to the table?" Ulukaya was proud of saying that no one could run his company better than he could, without any highly experienced professionals at the helm. He felt no need to bolster himself or his team. When his competitors brought their first batches of Greek yogurt to the market, Ulukaya said he was concerned but that upon trying the product, his worry proved unnecessary. "When I first tasted one of their yogurts, it was so terrible I thought it must have spoiled. I even wondered whether the company might deliberately be making its Greek yogurt taste terrible in an attempt to turn off consumers and spoil the entire category in order to preserve the profits of its established brands." So far, Chobani was safe.[21]

However, the company started to run into product-quality problems itself. In late 2012, Chobani had opened a $450 million, state-of-the-art yogurt factory in Twin Falls, Idaho, almost two thousand miles from headquarters. When customers started complaining about fizzy yogurt and bloated packaging, the company announced a large-scale recall. Grocers became impatient with the company and decreased shelf space. Competitors such as Danone SA and Yoplait aggressively expanded their offerings. As a result, Chobani's sales slipped, operating losses swung to over $115 million in the second half of 2013, and the company was saddled with over $700 million in debt. Accordingly, Ulukaya changed course. He brought on the mega-private-equity firm TPG with its deep pockets and industry connections to help right-size the company. In the three months following the product recall, Chobani hired three experienced personnel, including a chief financial officer and supply chain officer, each with at least eighteen years of experience. Ulukaya said, "I should've changed the people in those positions 3 or 4 times in the time we went from $0 to $1 billion. But I didn't change anything, because they were awesome people."[22]

Let's step back from Ulukaya's story to see the broader pattern. As an endeavor expands or takes on more complexity, the people responsible for its initial success will often have difficulty performing at the next level. We are inclined to show tremendous loyalty to the colleagues who helped us launch the endeavor. At that early stage, the emphasis is usually on flexible people who can perform multiple functions—even if they can't carry out any particularly well. With success and growth, the endeavor's challenges often heighten the need for excellence within specific functions, outweighing the need for flexibility, and those challenges rapidly outgrow the capabilities of the early participants. But leaders are slow to upgrade the team as the endeavor reaches its next stage of development, and the faster the success, the more intense the conflict. The head is saying to replace the early compatriots, but the heart is putting up powerful resistance. "What? Replace the people who got us here? They are awesome people!" It's a very different version of the Peter Principle: It's not that the people have moved up in a stable organization, as per the classical Principle, but that the organization has changed in ways that have outstripped their capabilities, even if they are playing the same role as before.

These are tough perils of success for anyone and are quite puzzling initially (and jarring for the person who succumbs to those perils). I first noticed these perils when I studied and analyzed more than two hundred startups. Founder-CEOs who had succeeded at completing the difficult task of developing their all-important first products also had significantly *higher* chances of being replaced as CEO. Essentially, until the product is developed, the technical or scientific cofounder is the best person to lead the charge. However, once the product is developed and is ready to be sold to customers, the company's challenges change dramatically. The technical project has to become a company. The project team has to work together with a sales team. The CEO has to build, lead, and knit together multiple functions. The technical or scientific founder usually has no experience in these new functions and thus doesn't even know how to interview potential hires into those functions, let alone manage and integrate them. The qualitative changes in these demands turn the founder's early strong suit into a liability. When these changes hit, even the smartest technical or scientific founder faces a steep learning curve that will slow down or even imperil the startup.

When it comes to self-awareness, people who succeed quickly often have the heightened challenge that Ulukaya faced: Their own success can further blind them to the signs that success might become a challenge, instead reinforcing the feeling that they have the game all figured out. Ulukaya had made it into a select group of founders, those who keep leading their company to further success even after fast growth. Yet, even though we can all come up with the names of a few founders who did likewise, they are well known precisely because they are the extreme exceptions.[23] Far more often, the successful founder is blindsided by the challenges of success, as was Ulukaya.

These perils of success apply to many areas of our lives. We often dive into a new task with a passion to excel and to climb to the next rung on the ladder. We are thrilled when we achieve that goal. However, often the next rung on the ladder brings challenges for which we haven't prepared adequately, transforming the realization of our fondest dream into the beginning of a nightmare.

The challenges posed by success are starkest when they are qualitatively different from the ones we faced until now. In a startup, the challenges of creation are replaced by the challenges of growth, one requiring a talent for leadership and the other a talent for operations. In a project, the challenges of achieving a design milestone distract us from the new, tougher problem of implementing the design. In family life, we elatedly graduate from one stage only to find unexpected discouragement at the next. For example, one family rented an apartment for years but dreamed of buying a house and proactively saved for a down payment. After months of visiting open houses, they found what they were looking for, negotiated and signed the purchase and sale agreement, and excitedly packed up for their move. They were ready to live their dream! However, their housing honeymoon didn't last for long. They discovered that they didn't like having to worry about the lawn, the flood-prone basement, the daily fines when they didn't shovel the sidewalk, the missing shingles on the roof, and the tree that needed to be removed before it came down on their car—and they didn't have the skills or inclination to take care of them themselves. They weren't prepared for the ceaseless charges for taxes, water, maintenance, and garbage collection. They longed for a return to the simple life of a tenant.

Success had bred its own challenges for them, ones for which they had neglected to prepare even as they had driven forward single-mindedly to achieve that success. Unfortunately, leaving home ownership had now become a lot harder for them. Hitting the "Undo" key on their decision had become a much more expensive endeavor. For one thing, they now had to unload their house, with the associated realtor fees and moving costs. They had succeeded, but unproductively, and they were in a worse place than if they had not succeeded at moving out of their apartment. As we see next, they, and Hamdi Ulukaya, could benefit from the lessons learned by founders whose approaches to achieving milestones had also enabled them to set the table for continued success rather than temporary accomplishment.

Pause for Reflection

- Have you ever been promoted into a position you long desired and then found that you were in over your head and unprepared for the new role?

  - Outside work, has a team on which you played made it to the playoffs and then found that it was unprepared for the heightened level of competition that came with that achievement?

  - Back when you applied to schools, were you admitted to your dream school but then worried about (or found out) that you might not have been prepared for the high level of performance required to succeed at it?

- In any of these situations, were there ways in which you could have prepared better, so that your success would have been more sustainable?

SUCCESS AT WORK AND FAILURE IN LIFE?

For founder Phil Knight of Nike, by the late 1970s his firm had become one of the largest athletic apparel companies in the United States. However, it was still being run by an executive team made up of Knight and his friends. Meetings were raucous, and disagreements had a tendency to escalate quickly into expletive-laden tirades. The chaos became palpable. Knight knew he needed to professionalize the company, but he struggled to assert control over his key people. On a business trip to Maine, one senior manager bought an entire factory without authorization from Knight. The director of marketing, Rob Strasser, followed suit by taking a product line to market too quickly, resulting in thousands of returns and damage to the Nike brand. Strasser and other key managers ended up divorced. While helping drive Nike's success, they had spent so much time away from home that their wives were sent T-shirts from the company bearing the heading "Nike Widow." Even Knight's wife filed, but later withdrew, divorce papers.[24]

We often think of our business lives as being separate from our personal lives. When things aren't going well at work, at least when we walk in the door at home, we still have our youngest charging up to us with arms wide open and an excited, "Mommy's home!" When things are going smashingly well at work, we might walk in the door only to have to deal with lingering family challenges. If only success in one domain could carry over to the other!

Nike's professional success resulted in Nike Widows. Likewise, Hamdi Ulukaya's initial success at Chobani exacerbated personal problems. Back in the late 1990s during his early days of becoming an entrepreneur, Ulukaya was married for two years to pediatrician Ayse Giray. In 2012, after Chobani had become a billion-dollar business, Giray sued Ulukaya for 53 percent of the company, claiming that she had provided the capital to fund Chobani's predecessor company and that they had a handwritten note documenting their agreement.[25] The $530 million lawsuit dragged on for three years. Just before the judge was due to rule on the case, Ulukaya agreed on a settlement. Had

Chobani not been a success, it is doubtful that Giray would have tried to lay claim to its ownership. Instead, Ulukaya's visible success had led to personal challenges that wouldn't have occurred otherwise.

In our most-cherished areas of life, we aspire to go from strength to strength, while avoiding going from failure to failure. As we next explore, the best practices of founders help us see how to also go from failure to strength, while avoiding going from strength to failure. Their approaches can help us make the best of those paths more likely and productive and the worst of those paths less likely and less devastating.

CHAPTER 4

FAIL AND SUCCEED PRODUCTIVELY

IT'S NO SECRET that there is a high rate of failure among startups and that the best entrepreneurs value failure and turn it to their advantage. Yet few of us have heard about how they do that or explored whether we can learn from and adopt any of founders' best practices in our lives. In the first half of this chapter, we delve into how entrepreneurs increase the chances that their failures will be productive. In the second half of the chapter, we examine the signs that should tip us off when success might actually be setting us up for failure. Even thinking of success and failure in these terms will be a shift for some of us. But there is a lot of sense in this mind-bending approach. And we soon see how to apply entrepreneurial best practices to help us anticipate and avoid the problems of both failure and success.

FAIL PRODUCTIVELY

At one level, the entrepreneurial approach to failure turns negative experiences into productive learning *after* failure occurs. Rather than seizing on successes and ignoring failures, entrepreneurs seize the opportunity introduced by failure. This approach was captured in one of the greatest TV commercials of all time, which featured Michael Jordan, arguably the best basketball player of all time, reflecting on his career: "I've missed more than nine thousand shots in my career. I've lost almost three hundred games. Twenty-six times I've been trusted to take the game-winning shot and missed. I've failed over and over and over again in my life. And that is why I succeed."[1] However, an even better entrepreneurial approach is to understand the value of failure *before* it occurs, when we can set up safety nets that enable us to continue unimpeded (regardless of a specific win or loss) or, in the best case, gain strength from our failures.

Harness Failure to Gain Strength
Rather than Lose Motivation

When we fail in pursuit of a goal, we tend to lose motivation to achieve it. However, great entrepreneurs build up resilience by recasting the meaning of failure. They frame it as a rite of passage rather than a personal breakdown, thereby minimizing the element of moral judgment, which can be paralyzing. As serial entrepreneur Andy Sparks learned from the ups and downs of his startup life, "Life is a series of focused and purposeful battles. It's about knowing each battle is part of a larger war to achieve whatever it is you want to achieve. But, in war, the eventual victor doesn't necessarily win all of the battles."[2]

This is one meaning behind the Talmudic phrase "Gam zu l'tova" (This is also for the best), which encourages individuals to view setbacks positively. One of the classic stories about the phrase involved the great sage Akiva, who was trying to reach a city before nightfall but found himself stuck in the woods when dark came. He dismounted from his donkey and lit his lone candle to pierce the darkness. However, the candle blew out, leaving him in the dark. Soon after, his donkey was killed by a wild animal.

Despite being alone in the dark and distant from his intended lodgings, Akiva at each step declared that the apparent disaster must be for the best. When he awoke the next morning, he walked to the city he was journeying toward only to find that it had been attacked overnight by a vicious band of marauders who had passed through the forest in which he had been staying. If they had seen his candle or heard his donkey bray, he would have likewise been attacked. Furthermore, if he had made it to town before nightfall, his fate would likely have been dreadful.[3]

Thus, in its original incarnation, "Gam zu l'tova" was an optimistic declaration of faith when faced by apparent disaster. However, it should also be an entrepreneurial charge to each of us, an exhortation to seize seemingly negative events and harness them—to use them as a way to rethink our paths in life or to reflect on learnings that can be used to improve our next steps. Setbacks should prompt us to ask: Is there any way in which this seemingly adverse development might result in a better outcome than the one I had been hoping to achieve? If so, what can I do to increase the likelihood of achieving that better outcome?

Years ago, a sentence from a student paper was so thought provoking that I put it up on my office wall: "It's easy to get stuck in a rut, especially if you're good at what you do." Often when we are on autopilot, a seemingly negative event is exactly what we need to force us to reflect on whether we're in a rut from which we needed an external push, or to fire up our motivation to get past barriers in our path.

Colin Hodge was unexpectedly facing such a barrier after founding a dating site in which people could find friends of friends who might be compatible with them. He had built a web application within Facebook and began garnering initial attention from users and the media. Hodge was approached by a venture capitalist from IDG Ventures who offered to invest $300,000. Hodge said, "They were super excited with what we were doing." Amid the discussion with IDG, Hodge and his cofounders competed in the prominent South-by-Southwest competition and emerged as winners, gaining a flurry of further attention. They returned home confident in their plans and the timing with which they were pursuing them. However, they were greeted by news from the venture capitalist: His firm didn't want to invest after all. "They said, 'We don't have faith that your popularity [on the web] is going to transfer to mobile.' . . . You think you have something in your hand, and then they take it from you."[4]

Over the preceding decade, Hodge had developed a mind-set that helped him heighten his motivation when confronted with negative developments: "Take a moment to process it, and get back to work, because you have to prove them wrong. Use that as a motivator! Anybody who says your idea won't work or your company won't work or you're going to fail at something or it's too hard, too risky—I use that as my personal motivation." He used the thumbs down from the investor to fire up his team and accelerate their plans to introduce a mobile version. Only a month after getting turned down, they launched on mobile and soon after were ranked in the top ten of mobile applications. Reflecting on it afterward, Hodge said, "With my personal goals and why am I doing this, a consistent pattern is that someone turned us down and said, 'This isn't going to work.' It is motivating! Sometimes you need external factors to rally your heart and push to prove them wrong."[5]

Founders who have trouble recovering from failure do not last long within entrepreneurial ventures. Those who do fail productively are often able to turn those bumps in the road into a smoother, higher-impact ride in their subsequent ventures. For instance, Texas executive Barry Nalls, whose experiences founding telecom-services company Masergy are described in Chapter 2, had founded a startup thirteen years before Masergy. After a decade of working for GTE, he decided that it was time to tap his wealth of business experience to start a consulting business. This startup would help small businesses convert their paper-based processes for handling accounts payable, accounts receivable, and payroll into electronic processes. He had grown up in a family of small-business founders who had started their companies with little planning, and Nalls did likewise. He said, "My planning for it was a scribbled one-page: 'Here's how much money I think I can make. Here's what I think my costs will be.' I only had a month or two of savings. . . . We had to make it from paycheck to paycheck. We had no safety net." Taking any project that came along, he ended up repairing rodeo timers and replacing light bulbs in the electronic signs atop car dealerships. After a year of working seven days a week and having a bank account with zero dollars in it, Nalls shut down the business and returned to GTE.[6]

What he did next is critical: Rather than licking his wounds and giving up on becoming an entrepreneur, Nalls spent the next few years addressing the weaknesses that had caused trouble for his consulting business. He realized that despite his apparent wealth of work experience, he didn't know how to start a business, how to raise money, or how to use that capital to build his company. He realized that he had to put even more thought and planning into his own startup than he did into each new project at GTE, which was considerable. He sought new job assignments within GTE that would help build a foundation for becoming a founder. For instance, he spent five years doing product management, one of the best training grounds for becoming an entrepreneur. He was determined to maintain focus on the projects or products he was developing rather than taking any project that came along. He also developed a much better prefounding financial cushion for himself and his family. When Nalls finally decided to return to entrepreneurship, he was far better armed to found a successful startup than he had been at first.[7]

When most of us experience failure, it is natural to be taken aback. Indeed, Nalls recoiled at first. (Imagine the "told you so" daggers he got on his first day back at GTE after his consulting firm failed!) However, engineer that he was, he saw his initial founding attempt as an experiment that yielded data for him, much like we saw above with basketball great Michael Jordan's reflections on the role of failure in his success, and much like Thomas Edison's perspective on his thousands of failed attempts at creating a light bulb: "I have not failed. I've just found 10,000 ways that won't work."[8] Nalls converted the dark days of failure into a productive failure by learning from his experiences and using those lessons to act differently in the next stage. How can we tell if our failure has been productive? It is productive if we attempt a similar project and then can point to significant changes we made because of the lessons we learned, as did Nalls.

We might say that Tommy John was an entrepreneurial thinker with a world-class pitching arm, because he is a model of harnessing failure to gain strength. John was a natural athlete. A standout basketball player in his home state of Indiana, he held his city's single-game scoring record. He also found baseball a natural sport and was signed by the Cleveland Indians. He made his major league pitching debut in 1963 at the tender age of twenty years old.

Over his first decade in the league, John was a middling pitcher, winning only 52 percent of his games. He began the 1974 season pitching for the Dodgers with an excellent 13–3 record, though, winning his first-ever player of the month award. He was on top of the world. Then, on July 17, 1974, in the middle of a game, John suffered a devastating injury, tearing the ulnar collateral ligament in his pitching arm. He said, "I had runners on first and second. I was trying to get the batter . . . to hit a ground ball so I could get out of the inning unscathed. Right as I threw, I felt this searing pain . . . and I went, 'Holy mackerel, what did I do?'" He tried to throw another pitch, without success. "I got to the bench, I got my jacket. I told our trainer, I said, 'Billy, let's get Dr. Jobe—something's wrong.'"[9]

Frank Jobe, the Dodgers' orthopedic surgeon who was also a good friend of John, had to give him the bad news: His baseball career was over. He would never pitch again; his arm was crippled by the tear. "If I were you, Tommy, I'd think about another line of work."[10] To help John recover some functionality, Jobe proposed a surgery that had never been attempted, in which he would take a tendon from his right forearm and graft it onto his left elbow. Jobe gave the surgery a 1 percent chance of success and described the risks it introduced.

"Well, I was valedictorian of my high school class," John said, "and 1 percent or 2 percent in 100 is far better than 0 percent in 100." Dr. Jobe performed the surgery on September 25, 1974. John had taken a calculated risk, but things took a turn for the worse. The surgery left him with a "claw hand" and extremely limited mobility. He required another surgery to repair nerve damage, extending his recovery period.

John had gone from invincible to incapacitated in a split second. This is the kind of plunge that destroys most people's optimism and can test even the most confident entrepreneur. They lose the mental energy needed to spring back to who and what they were and to face the unappealing choices that so often arise after a major setback.

Things got even worse for John. He soon began losing the feeling in his hand; it felt asleep and cold. So he ran it under hot water to stimulate the circulation. On his next weekly visit to Dr. Jobe, the doctor noticed a burn on his hand. John had lost so much feeling that he hadn't been able to feel that the water was scalding hot! An electromyography scan showed that John had suffered severe nerve damage and required a third surgery, which Dr. Jobe performed in December. John's wife, Sally, was shocked when she saw his shriveled hand and began to suffer from feelings of panic and depression.[11]

The natural athlete found that simple tasks had become huge mountains to climb. He dropped forks of food and had to teach himself how to eat, how to brush his hair, and how to sign a check with his weaker hand.

We could all understand if John were tempted to treat himself to marathon TV sessions while eating his favorite treats and mourning the end of his career just as it was reaching its peak. Instead, he decided, "The operation is over—now it's up to me. I've got to do it from here on out."[12] He drew strength from two major inspirations: his first child, Tamara, who was born the same month as his first surgery, and biblical stories. For instance, John recounted hearing that "in Genesis eighteen, Abraham—over a hundred years old—tells his wife, Sarah, some eighty years old, that God promised them a child. Think of the impossibility of that situation. What a cruel hoax—a *baby*—at their age? But God promised—and Abraham says to Sarah, 'Is anything too hard for the Lord?'"[13]

He developed a grueling rehabilitation schedule that had him practicing, pain or not, every day except Sunday. As his biographer recounts, "Tommy was tougher on himself than ever before. He ran farther than before, did more knee bends, exercised longer and harder, lifted more weights than he ever had before."[14] For months there was little sign of progress. One day when spending time with his former teammates, John overheard one comment: "The guy should be realistic. . . . He's finished. Why doesn't he face up to it?"[15]

After several months of painstaking work, John was able to throw a baseball—but not well, and certainly not with the precision and power it would take to return to the major leagues. John worked with teammate and major league pitcher Mike Marshall, who had a PhD in kinesiology and an ability to help pitchers recover from injuries. Marshall taught John a completely different way to pitch in which he would not turn his leg and would instead go straight to the plate, which reduced the chance of hurting his knee and arm. John also recruited the Dodgers' masseur, who spent dozens of hours massaging his shoulder, arm, and hand.

As his feeling slowly returned and his pitches improved, John asked the Dodgers to assign him to the Instructional League, where young prospects early in their minor-league careers played. There, he continued to refine his new pitching motion and build up his strength. John eventually returned to the Dodgers for the 1976 season. He recounted to his father that, "The first half of the season was a learning process: I had to learn or relearn so many little things about batters, mechanics of pitching, and the like. It was almost like starting over."[16] His 10–10 record that year was considered miraculous. In his second year after returning from the surgery, he won twenty games, a stellar accomplishment for any starting pitcher and one he had never approached presurgery. That year, he came in second in the Cy Young Award voting for best pitcher in the league. He went on to win more than twenty games in three out of those four postsurgery years, making the all-star team for three straight years.

John pitched until 1989, with well over half of his 288 career wins coming after his surgery. Even though it had looked like his career was over after only a decade in the league, in 1989 John tied the record for most seasons played in a major league baseball career, with twenty-six seasons. That same year, John decided it was time to retire when Mark McGwire, the son of John's dentist, got two hits off him. John said of his decision, "When your dentist's kid starts hitting you, it's time."[17]

Hundreds—if not thousands—of pitchers have had what is now called Tommy John surgery. John remains a symbol of one who has faced certain failure and came back even stronger and more resilient for the experience.

Just as Tommy John seized on his two biggest areas of inspiration, his faith and his family, to gain strength from his setback, we should also seek at least one source of motivation to anchor us. One of those sources may be the very setback that we had; witness Colin Hodge's heightened motivation after his rejection by IDG Ventures. When we get turned down for a promotion, don't get hired by the company at the top of our list, or come in second in a contest we thought we deserved to win, we shouldn't try to eliminate the feelings of disappointment. Instead, we should harness them. In fact, for certain tasks and goals, harnessing our setbacks may be even more effective than trying to build on an interim success. Hebrew University psychologist Maya Tamir and her colleagues have shown that for making progress toward a goal, negative emotions can be more useful than positive ones. For instance, in confrontational situations, angry people—those who were feeling the righteous indignation of having a chip on their shoulder—performed better than people who felt good.[18] Gaining motivation to prove wrong the company that didn't promote or hire us, the publisher who turned down our manuscript, or the judges who didn't give us the gold medal can enable us to reach heights of impact that we might not have reached otherwise.

Turning setbacks into blessings is a skill and a mind-set that we would do best to practice before we really need to tap it. Rather than waiting for a real failure from which we have to recover, take small bumps in the road as opportunities to learn and to practice Tommy John's and Barry Nalls's approaches. Practice reframing your outlook by seeing failure as a learning step toward future achievement. One thought-provoking metaphor for the perspectives we might adopt: Do we view our path through life as an obstacle course, or as a treasure hunt? Is every challenge a difficult barrier to surmount, or an opportunity to pick up a new experience that could prove valuable for helping us reach our ultimate goal? When we encounter a failure, do we view ourselves as *stuck*, or as *positioned to improve* because of the experience? Having built this recovery muscle using our small bumps, it will be stronger and more habitual when we really need it.

Learning from our failures helps make failure less likely, as does the way in which we attribute the failure. Marty Seligman of the University of Pennsylvania found that the single best predictor of success for salespeople—a group subjected to constant rejection, and a group whose core sales skill is critical to founders who have to achieve buy-in from a wide variety of people and organizations—is how they explain failure to themselves and others. The best do so in a style that allows them to move forward without being personally humiliated.[19] When a sales prospect says no to them, rather than feeling helpless or deciding "I am no good at this job; I can't sell this product," they delve into the causes in order to gain new insights. They ask why the prospect didn't bite and may find that "my customer doesn't need this right now" rather than blaming themselves, harming their motivation, and inhibiting their ability to learn from the situation. Note that this isn't the same as avoiding responsibility; the best salespeople freely accept responsibility for their setbacks but speak pragmatically about them, avoiding the tendency to see problems as personal, pervasive, or permanent.[20] They don't allow setbacks to define them. The key is to adopt a growth mind-set in which you see yourself as constantly developing, rather than as a fixed persona,[21] so that a failure represents not a judgment of your essence or potential but a step toward your continued improvement.

Once you've acquired the knowledge that comes with a setback, you're a more valuable contributor than you were before—and more valuable than people who never gained that knowledge. You may have incurred a stiff tuition bill for those hard life lessons, but you're better educated than the people who haven't paid tuition yet.

Find Something to Appreciate, Even During the Dark Days

Some events are too devastating for us to turn into "Gam zu l'tova" recoveries. Even for those, though, we have to find ways to recover and get back onto a productive path.

For instance, Sheryl Sandberg had been hired as the chief operating officer of fast-growing startup Facebook in 2008 and was on top of the world, having been named every year since 2007 to *Fortune* magazine's "50 Most Powerful Women in Business" list. She had been happily married since 2004 to Dave Goldberg, the CEO of private online-data company SurveyMonkey, and had a son and a daughter.

On May 1, 2015, while they were on vacation in Mexico, Goldberg died, reportedly of a heart problem while using a treadmill.[22]

In a 2016 commencement address at the University of California, Berkeley, Sandberg reflected on the mentors who helped her find something to appreciate even during the dark days after Goldberg's death: "One day my friend Adam Grant, a psychologist, suggested that I think about how much worse things could be. This was completely counterintuitive; it seemed like the way to recover was to try to find positive thoughts. 'Worse?' I said. 'Are you crazy? How could things be worse?' His answer cut straight through me: 'Dave could have had that same cardiac arrhythmia while he was driving your children.' Wow. The moment he said it, I felt overwhelming gratitude that my family was alive. That gratitude overtook some of the grief."[23]

She continued with the daily habits she has adopted to help instill the attribute of gratitude: "Finding gratitude and appreciation is key to resilience. People who take the time to list things they are grateful for are happier and healthier. It turns out that counting your blessings can actually increase your blessings. My New Year's resolution this year is to write down three moments of joy before I go to bed each night. This simple practice has changed my life. Because no matter what happens each day, I go to sleep thinking of something cheerful."[24]

For too many people, Thanksgiving is just one day each year. For the resilient, thanksgiving is a constant companion they foster, helping them deal with even the worst of developments. Whether it's taking two minutes each night to write down three things for which you were thankful today, or going around the family dinner table each Friday night to hear one gem of appreciation from each member of the family—or being a founder at a company meeting after a round of financing falls through, asking her team what blessings might come from not having raised the capital—proactively build your appreciation muscle and those of the people around you so thanksgiving can become a habit that will strengthen you in the face of loss or failure.[25]

Avoid Overpersisting and Digging a Deeper Hole

Before we move from recovering productively from a setback to proactively planning for one, an important caution about developing a setback-tolerant attitude: Don't overpersist through failures. Advice columnist Ann Landers reportedly said: "Some people believe holding on and hanging in there are signs of great strength. However, there are times when it takes much more strength to know when to let go and then do it."[26] Entrepreneurs are conditioned by countless articles, books, and anecdotes to think that there is only virtue in persistence, but overpersisting can cost them dearly.

Tim Westergren, founder in 1999 of online-music startup Savage Beast, was lauded by a prominent blogger as "the poster child for startup persistence" after enduring three hundred rejections from potential investors, a lawsuit from employees, and a "divorce" from his cofounder.[27] Then came the crippling blow: Congress intended to dramatically hike the royalties that Savage Beast would have to pay to music companies. A full decade after founding—during what should have been the prime of his life—all Westergren had to show for his persistence was a severely hamstrung company. The homespun advice of columnist Ann Landers might have served him well.

Interestingly, a dozen years after founding, Savage Beast, now called Pandora Radio, went public. However, despite his painful dozen years of building the company, Westergren was left with only 2.4 percent of the company at the time, in contrast to the more than 75 percent held by the venture capitalists.

Even the initial public offering was bittersweet, as major competitors such as Spotify and Apple by then offered virtually identical streaming services.

When I teach my case study about Westergren, the students are divided over whether he was wise or foolish to have stuck with it as long as he did, even after seeing the company's eventual success. The decade-plus ordeal was hard on his relationships and his health (the case study opens with Westergren being awakened at 4:00 a.m. with stress-induced chest pains). One of my students asked: If Westergren's company had ultimately failed, "would we call the protagonist's 'persistence' just an addiction?"

When the world is falling in on us, as it was for Westergren for quite a long time, will we be able to evaluate clearly and dispassionately whether our persistence is becoming destructive? In trying to erase deep losses, will we go to extremes that only exacerbate the situation?[28] Instead of exposing ourselves to that danger, we should heed the Chinese proverb that says, "If you must play, decide on three things at the start: the rules of the game, the stakes, and the quitting time," and then act if it's time to fold our hand.[29]

Proactively Plan for the "Undo" Key

So far, our best practices have all focused on recovery. However, a key element of entrepreneurs' ability to deal productively with failure is their *proactive* approach to identifying decisions for which it will be hard to "hit the Undo key" and creating forward-looking plans that can be reversed more easily after missteps.

For instance, an early founding decision for which it is hard to hit the Undo key is when the founders of a company decide how to divide the ownership of the company among themselves. A classic cautionary tale comes from the founders of the pioneering Zipcar car-sharing service. Early in the company's life, the two founders discussed how to split the company's equity ownership among themselves and quickly shook hands on an "easy" 50-50 split. As is typical of the majority of founding teams in my research, this early split was set in stone, meant to last throughout the life of the startup. Robin Chase, one of the cofounders, threw herself into building the company and pushed forward almost every element of the business. Her cofounder, on the other hand, decided to contribute only from the sidelines while keeping her day job.

When Chase talked to my class about their equity split, she called it "a really stupid handshake" because she couldn't easily hit the Undo key on that early arrangement, legally, financially, and interpersonally. The fact that her cofounder was benefiting equally from Chase's hard work "caused [Chase] a huge amount of angst" for years. Likewise, think about the interpersonal and legal ulcers Mark Zuckerberg caused for himself because of an ill-advised early equity split with his Facebook cofounder that was difficult to undo, even with the best legal assistance. (If not for the difficulty of undoing their equity arrangement, the movie *The Social Network* would never have been made!) Similar mistakes come from ill-structured marital prenuptial agreements (or not adopting a prenup when one was needed) and from joint ventures between companies that become very hard to unwind when one of the parties wants to secede from the partnership.

The founding team of Ockham Technologies took a far better, proactive approach to splitting their company's equity. Ockham had been sparked by Ken Burows, an experienced consultant in the sales-compensation industry who saw an opportunity to create computer systems to automate the compensation process. But Burows's two cofounders had doubts about whether he would leave his day job to join Ockham; he had just become a father and was enjoying his stable, full-time job. If he walked away with his shares, the company would be unable to use his ownership portion to attract a high-quality replacement.[30]

It was a difficult conversation; Burows was the cofounders' friend, the person who had brought them into Ockham, and the whole reason the company existed. They raised their doubts and ended up discussing three starkly different scenarios: In one, Burows would come aboard full time (best-case scenario); in the second, he would work part time on nights and weekends while keeping his day job (expected-case scenario); in the third, he would not work at all for Ockham because of the demands of fatherhood and his job (worst-case scenario). For each scenario, they agreed on what the resulting ownership amounts would be, providing a much more robust way to deal with what could have been a devastating occurrence. When Burows did, in fact, decide not to leave his day job, Ockham was well prepared to deal with that setback.[31]

Unlike Robin Chase, who had to suffer years of pain because of her strikingly similar, hard-to-undo mistake, the proactive founders of Ockham were able to hit the Undo key after anticipating the need to craft a very different type of agreement. They reclaimed Burows's ownership stake and redeployed it to people who had full (and full-time) dedication to the startup, forging a stronger team despite—nay, because of—the setback of his departure.

At its core, the Ockham team built a process, like those described in Nassim Nicholas Taleb's book *Antifragile*, that improved with failure rather than being defeated by it.[32] The worst-case scenario is a fragile system that falls apart when hit by a shock. Far better is a resilient system that withstands the shock and remains the same as before. The best is an antifragile system that *improves* as a result of the shock. The human body is a great example of antifragility: Immune systems become more robust when exposed to small doses of germs, and muscles become stronger, not weaker, when exposed to stress (or exercise)— unless, of course, they're stressed too much, as happened in Tommy John's case.

In general, one of the critical underpinnings of antifragility is that mistakes need to be small and isolated enough that the overall system survives and has a chance to grow stronger. Among manufactured systems, Taleb points to aviation safety. One (small, isolated) plane crash provides the aviation system with critical information about what went wrong so that the system can adapt and improve, thereby lessening the risk of a more catastrophic crash. Also, "good systems, such as airlines, are set up to have small errors that are independent from each other—or in effect, negatively correlated to each other, since mistakes lower the odds of future mistakes."[33] Contrast this with the modern banking system, where one failure makes another system failure even *more* likely to occur.

These examples may seem far afield from your own decisions, but they can be easily applied. For instance, if you're taking a job in a new city, rent there before you buy, or consider commuting for a while; even if the rent seems like money down the drain and the long-distance commuting is a pain, there's a benefit to what you'll learn while being able to reverse the decision if the job isn't quite what you want. At the same time, do not underestimate the barriers that might get in the way of setting up Undo keys. For one, we have a tendency to plan for the best scenario and to neglect the need to plan for the worst cases. For example, only 3 percent of Americans get a prenuptial agreement, even though 50 percent of American marriages end in divorce. Another excuse people use for not anticipating and avoiding problems is the idea that putting in place a backup plan may reduce their drive to achieve their initial plan. Some experimental, lab-based evidence suggests that reduced motivation may be a valid concern,[34] but for potentially harmful failures, the value of an insurance policy can far outweigh marginally reduced motivation.

Overcoming these psychological barriers can be somewhat easier if big decisions can be broken down into smaller ones. For Ockham's founders, a general feeling of "We face a lot of risks" prompted them to analyze and prioritize the specific risks and led them to the conclusion that the best approach was to act quickly on their biggest risk. Similarly, when beginning an endeavor, work ahead of time to transform failure into a productive experience. From the beginning, set modest expectations to make it easier to consider potential pitfalls. Force realistic viewpoints on yourself to protect yourself from outside hype based on best-case scenarios. Proceed gradually, breaking big decisions into a series of smaller ones, and when moves go poorly, develop a habit of actively reflecting, learning, and adapting.

By doing so, you'll proactively remove some of the failures that you might have faced otherwise, and you'll build the antifragility muscles necessary to harness failure for the better when it does hit. But what if you succeed?

ANTICIPATE THE CHALLENGES OF SUCCESS

Let's say you succeed beyond your wildest dreams. After being cooped up in a small apartment for several years, you decide to buy a house for your growing family and fall in love with one that would be perfect for you. To make sure you get it, you submit a bid at or above the asking price (after all, it's just inside the maximum mortgage for which you were approved) and are delighted to have your bid accepted. Or you get accepted off the wait list to your dream college or graduate school, which is known for its academic rigor. Or you get an offer to come into an established company at a level two steps higher than your current position (and two rungs on the salary ladder higher). "Yes!" you respond excitedly. You can't wait to jump right into your new life. After all, this result is everything you've dreamed of, right?

Not so fast; it's time to pull back on the reins. There are several other steps to take first, including some that might lead you to consider refusing that promotion or acceptance.

All of us want to succeed. However, sometimes achieving those goals can have negative ramifications for us—ramifications for which we are unprepared. Many entrepreneurs fail to prepare for success. This can be surprising, given that so many of them possess an astonishing faith in their ability to build a company. If you truly believe you're going to reach your desired destination, wouldn't it make sense to think about what you'll need there? In theory, yes. But establishing a new path can be an overwhelming task, leaving us with little energy to worry about anything else. Nevertheless, it should be obvious that success will look very different from the struggle to survive. The best entrepreneurs have figured out how to anticipate the challenges of success and how to act so success doesn't become their demise.

Educate Yourself About the Potholes in the Road Ahead

Recall from Chapter 3 the challenges Hamdi Ulukaya faced because of his early success at Chobani: production and quality problems, a devastating product recall, skyrocketing debt and losses. Ulukaya, to his credit, changed course after running into these major problems. He brought in the mega-private-equity firm TPG, with its deep pockets and industry connections, to help right-size the company. In the three months following the product recall, Chobani hired three experienced personnel.[35] Ulukaya recovered, but he could have had a much smoother road had he had looked around the corner a lot earlier.

Remember how Barry Nalls harnessed the lessons from his initial failed endeavor and then test drove the idea of running a business from the passenger seat? For twenty years before he founded Masergy, Nalls sought work experiences that would prepare him: working for a large company to build his product-management skills, starting his own consulting firm to experience founding firsthand, and working for two startups before founding Masergy. He saw firsthand the challenges posed by growth and success.

As a result, his telecommunications startup, Masergy, developed proactive approaches for dealing with the need to transition from employees who can juggle many balls to specialization. When he hired an executive who would be a direct report to him, Nalls told me, he would proactively warn, "At some point in the future, I'll be hiring a boss for you. You'll have the ability to compete for the position, but someone else from outside the company could take the job." Nalls admitted, "Saying that doesn't quite work—we want aggressive people, and anyone aggressive wants to believe they can work at a higher level, but they usually don't scale." However, his proactive and repeated warnings helped ease the change when it came. Such statements might make it less attractive for an executive to come aboard, but Nalls knew it was likely he would have to hire experienced leadership within a few years to oversee his early hires and he wanted Masergy to avoid the debilitating effects of the Peter Principle.

Likewise, the best entrepreneurs map out upcoming business needs and prepare to fill their holes *before* the need hits. In a high-growth or capital-intensive business, proactively managing a company's upcoming needs likely entails seeking outside capital to fund expensive outside hires and expansion plans. After all, growth is exciting, until you notice that it is eating lots of your cash or outstripping your capabilities, as it did for Hamdi Ulukaya.

The lessons of unplanned success apply to other situations as well. Before you make a high-end offer for that dream house, stress-test your finances by analyzing worst-case scenarios and seeing if you can still afford the mortgage. Managers hiring for a team can also use these principles to prepare for success. Besides setting proper expectations for change over time, they can map candidates onto a chart of the team's needs, both now and in the next stage of development. What is my checklist of the capabilities we need now and how does this person fit into it? How is the checklist likely to change in six or twelve months and would this person still fit? In considering candidates, they can envision negative as well as positive scenarios in order to assess the risks that each hire involves. Echoing the advice from Chapter 2, where possible, "try before buying" by bringing in candidates as contractors for short projects. Unlike Ulukaya, who admits that he kept—for far too long—his early employees who weren't growing fast enough as business boomed, don't let personal loyalty undermine the future of the business. As Ulukaya found, even if you *can* physically remove them, your ties to them will severely challenge your *want* to do so.

Take Control of the "Can" and the "Want"

Change heightens the potential for surprises, at two levels. The first is finding out too late that you can't perform as well in your new arena. In a new promotion, you've just traded in your old role (at which you excelled) for a new one, likely with significantly greater responsibility, perhaps with a different boss, or possibly managing new staff. The first year may be rocky as you grow into your new position. Your higher profile may require that you improve your leadership skills. If you relocate or switch industries, you'll need to build your credibility in new networks before you'll be able to tap it as well as your old network.

At the other level, even if you are confident that you have these capabilities and contacts to excel in the new arena—that you *can* lead—also reflect on whether you *want* to do so. To successfully navigate the unfamiliar (but welcome) terrain of success, it's key to maintain awareness of what drew you to helming your team in the first place. For instance, do your talents and passions lie in creating something from nothing, but not in refining an existing effort? If so, then focus on contributing during that early stage and then exiting before the next stage in favor of someone who excels at refining. Are you attracted by the chance to contribute to the organization or by the financial benefits of being a manager? In a study of 1,130 front-line managers, half of the managers took the role because it would lead to higher compensation.[36] However, compared to the 33 percent who took the role to make a greater contribution to the company, those for whom compensation was the major motivator were 57 percent more likely to become disillusioned by the job, having realized that the additional compensation was not enough to make up for the increased work hours and stress.

To assess these two levels when he was building an administrative team at the MassChallenge startup incubator, CEO John Harthorne first took potential employees as volunteers and watched how well they performed (the "can") and were motivated by his vision (the "want"). He explained to me that from the best of the volunteers he selected people to become paid interns. From the best of the interns, he selected the people who would become his full-time employees. At each stage, he watched carefully for signs of whether the employee could continue succeeding or whether the success of being promoted would cause problems, and whether the "want" was building or waning at each step. Thanks in part to disciplined practices like these, MassChallenge has become a huge startup incubator, helping build more than 125 startups each year in its Boston location alone.

If you realize that you are missing either the *can* or the *want*, seize the reins of change so you can play a role in defining what the change will look like and what your role might be after the change. For instance, founder-CEOs who initiate the process to bring in a new CEO to replace them end up with a much better landing spot than the founders whose boards or investors initiate the change. Founders who initiate the change are 20 percent more likely to remain at the company in a different position rather than unhappily leaving the company immediately. When the board initiates the change, founders who stay after being replaced are seven times more likely to receive a lower-level position than founders who stay after they initiated the change themselves. Founders who initiate the change are also much more likely to remain on the board of directors.[37] By having deeper self-awareness about their abilities and desires, they are able to get ahead of the curve and shape their futures, rather than having to react to someone else's decisions.

Try to shape your future—but be aware of the biases that can get in the way. According to psychologists Tim Wilson and Dan Gilbert, problems are caused during our goal setting when we "mis-want" something. We often make mistakes in our expectations of how good we will feel when we get something we want and of how long that feeling will last.[38] For instance, in one study, assistant professors believed that whether they received tenure would strongly influence their long-term happiness. Wilson and Gilbert assessed the actual happiness of two groups of professors who were several years ahead in their careers: former assistant professors who had received tenure and those who had not. They found that those who had failed to receive tenure were just as happy as those who had achieved it.[39] ("Gam zu l'tova" even applies to academic careers!) In the opposite direction, we often misjudge the negative effects we expect to experience from bad developments.

Wilson and Gilbert exhort people not to overestimate the heights of the good feelings and the depths of the bad ones or the duration for which each emotion will last. They suggest avoiding "focalism": "Consider the many other events that will inevitably unfold" at the same time as you are dealing with the focal event you experienced, and consider how those other events will moderate the extremes of the focal event.[40] Extreme heartache will be dampened by small, unexpected celebrations; extreme triumph by the daily bumps of life. Only once you have calibrated your wants are you ready to set your new goals.

This is not to say that we have to have a full picture of the future before we embark on any endeavor. We have to be ready to react productively to new developments even if we weren't fully prepared for them ahead of time. However, the fact that we cannot prepare for everything doesn't mean we should be blindsided by things we could have anticipated. As you embark on a new endeavor, learn about the broad outlines of the challenges you might face in later stages. Then, each step of the way, learn more deeply about the next stage and how you can get help tackling the challenges that will come with succeeding at getting to that stage.

Aggressively Bolster Your Support

When analysis shows that you are missing the skills needed to continue leading your project, committee, or company, your first reaction shouldn't be to leave the scene. The intangibles you bring to the endeavor will be sorely missed, and you will probably miss the impact that you could have had if you had stuck around. Similarly, when you get into that academically demanding dream school, don't let anxiety lead you to turn down your admission. Instead, focus on identifying the challenges for which you are not prepared and then explore how you might be able to bolster your support in those areas.

First, figure out if you have the time, desire, and capability to learn those new capabilities yourself. If you do, then find out from experts in those capabilities what the best resources and approaches are to learning about them. Before starting at your dream school, use the summer before you matriculate to strengthen your academic foundation and make sure you explore in advance what tutoring or academic-support services you might be able to tap. Second, for capabilities you wouldn't be able to learn, see if you can find people who already have those capabilities who might be interested in joining your effort, whether from the outside as a partner or advisor, or from the inside as an employee or board member. Armed with your knowledge of the holes you need to fill, negotiate with your potential new investor, company, or supervisor (or parents) to get money or people to add those skills and resources. By bolstering your support, you increase the chances that you can deal with the challenges of success while remaining at the helm.

At Chobani, once Ulukaya had realized the need to bolster his support, he did so at multiple levels of the organization. He attracted investor TPG, whose deep pockets and industry connections would fill two big holes. Within the executive team, he brought in senior executives with decades of experience in areas he lacked: supply chains and startup finance.

The same holds for the people below you who might be facing the challenges of success. Like John Harthorne of MassChallenge and Barry Nalls of Masergy, you too can better prepare your organization to withstand the demands of high growth. If you are an executive trying to develop and assess your employees, identify the biggest question marks that might get in the way of their being ready for a promotion, then give them the opportunity both to prove that they can address those question marks and to receive any developmental support needed to do so.

For instance, when Sharon McCollam was the chief financial officer of retailer Best Buy, one of her direct reports was Corie Barry, who had been hired in late 2012 and had become senior vice president of domestic finance. In August 2013, at a meeting with Barry, McCollam outlined specific issues that could get in the way of Barry's becoming her successor as CFO: Barry's lack of involvement in investor relations and other key areas and her ability "to take contradictory points of view during crucial conversations." Barry worked on those targeted areas while maintaining her strengths in others, and when McCollam left the CFO position, Barry was promoted to be her replacement in June 2016.[41]

Consider Refusing Your Admission

You have been offered admission to your dream school or have been offered a promotion. You have educated yourself about the potholes on the road ahead and have done everything you can to bolster your support in the areas with which you'll need help. Yet many upcoming problems still loom. Now think twice before saying yes to that wait-list admission or that promotion. Promotions are seductive but can also imperil success. For instance, research from human-resources consulting firm Development Dimensions International suggests that people who reluctantly accept a promotion into management (most often, they accepted it to get paid more but weren't keen on leading people) are twice as likely to end up quitting.[42] One-third of corporate managers regretted being promoted because they felt they were unprepared for the new position or did not understand how to succeed in it.[43] The new position might take you away from the parts of your job that have been most fulfilling, might require longer hours, and might come with unwelcome pressure to perform.

Academia provides a clear example of promotions imperiling success, both personal and organizational. Often, prolific academics are promoted to chair their departments. As a result, their research suffers at the same time as they may be heading toward committing leadership malpractice at the departmental level, given their lack of leadership capabilities and interests.

Instead, take a more conscious and self-aware approach to evaluating potential promotions. Be open to turning down promotions that are likely to become problematic or don't lend themselves to the best practices described above.

When I was leading the systems-integration practice I had founded back in the 1990s, the most consistently valuable contributor to our projects was a woman who was fifteen years older than I was and could have been playing a managerial role. However, she had long ago decided that remaining an individual contributor fit better with her likes and talents; she was much happier being an excellent individual contributor than having to manage a project team with the accompanying stress and need for travel. She had also recently given birth to twins, and moving up to a managerial role would have increased her workload beyond what she wanted to have while her children were young. So every time she was offered a managerial promotion, she refused it. I admired her self-awareness, the clarity of her priorities, and her ability to resist the flattering promotions that would have been her admission ticket into the world of management.

THINK DIFFERENTLY ABOUT SUCCESS AND FAILURE

As we have seen, our emotions often drive our decisions, and they don't always drive us to where we truly want or need to go. So if you sense that your emotions are leading you, watch out! Look for clues that your heart may be in control. Does the choice seem too easy? Does it feel too comfortable? Are you too passively giving in to your fears or desires?

The value of the entrepreneurial mind-set is that it flips our natural inclinations on their heads. Instead of our natural inclination to avoid failure and avidly seek success, the smartest entrepreneurs harness failure for the good and allocate time to think about how to manage the challenges of success. Doing so requires them to deepen their *self-awareness* about their capabilities and inclinations and about what they can control and change in themselves. It requires the humility necessary to tune into your weaknesses and diagnose when you might have to adjust your goals or ask for more support. It also requires *social awareness* of interpersonal dynamics and of the interests and motivations of those around us.

The art of doing this well requires us to adopt these practices, but in a very targeted way. For instance, creating Undo keys for every decision we make would be quite costly. Instead, which decisions would be most devastating if you couldn't undo a negative outcome? Which are most likely to result in that negative outcome? For the decisions that could become devastating and are relatively likely to occur, invest time and thought into how to plant Undo seeds now. Likewise, preparing for every possible downside of success will take a lot of time and may diminish our motivation to pursue that success. Instead, prioritize the downsides and act to reduce the issues introduced by the items at the top of your list. Your increased confidence that you can handle those downsides should help fire up your motivation rather than diminish it.

Looking to the next stage of entrepreneurial thinking, when we are making important changes in our lives, we tap the approaches, or blueprints, that have helped us succeed until now and apply them in our new arena. But our blindness to key differences between the old and new arenas can result in a disconnect between what worked for us in the past and what we need now. In the extreme, our past strengths can even become weaknesses. Shifting to a new arena can also surface key assumptions we didn't even know we were making, or natural inclinations that once seemed benign but could become disastrous now. Those inclinations include the desire to flock with birds of a feather, to involve friends and family in endeavors but avoid the difficult conversations necessary for productive collaboration, and to succumb to the magnetic pull of equality. Next, we learn how to apply founders' best practices for identifying the ingrained assumptions that can cause problems after we decide to make a change.

PART II

MANAGING A CHANGE

AS WE FOLLOW CAROLINE, Akhil, Barry, and others through their crises and turning points, we see the value of adopting entrepreneurs' strategies in multiple life areas. From learning when to leap to reducing your personal burn rate, or trying before you buy, each of these strategies is a variation on a single theme: Sometimes we need to pause, give up our reliance on familiar routines, and venture into uncomfortable territory.

The second half of this book is all about that part of your journey—the part in which you venture into the unknown having made a concrete decision. Broadly, this topic comes up constantly in my discussions with executives and students because many are at inflection points in their lives. They face high-stakes choices about whether to move toward greater or lesser comfort. Should they rely on gut feelings or take actions that feel strange and counterintuitive? Should they do what's expected or try something different?

I empathize with them, not only because I have gone through many of my own inflection points but also because I value my traditions and routines as much as the next person. Deviating from well-established patterns of thinking is never easy. But as we see in the following chapters, you are more likely to be on the right track if your decisions are stretching your ability to weigh your options rationally—if they are forcing you to think about the long term and face your fears, such as about others' possible disappointment in your choices.

As the chapters of this next part show, we can learn from founders to become more comfortable with the idea of rejecting, or at least objectively evaluating, commonplace wisdom. As we do, we become more comfortable with the unfamiliar and more familiar with discomfort.

Part II also further examines the idea that early choices make a big difference. Choices made in the early phase of a new initiative—whether it's a job, creative project, or marriage—bear fruit in the growth phase, as is the case in entrepreneurial firms. We look more closely at how to ensure that your new dreams, whatever they are, have a good chance to grow and thrive once you have invested in them.

CHAPTER 5

ARE YOU BLOCKED BY YOUR BLUEPRINT AND HOOKED ON ROUTINE?

AS BEINGS WHO ARE SHAPED for survival, we are adept at spotting the anomalous and surprising. In the distant past, it was the quick movements of prey. Now, it might be a new venture in a dull market or a drastic markdown of a sought-after product. Usually we are not concerned that this facility comes at the expense of our focus on what's ordinary and typical. If something is familiar, we happily tune it out. Have you ever driven to work without registering a single detail of the route? We habitually shut down our active thinking, routinizing our behaviors or defaulting to rules of thumb in order to save cognitive resources. That way, when something truly important happens—a new noise comes from the engine or a ball bounces through an intersection—we notice.

But, sometimes, conserving our cognitive resources gets us into trouble. When we face complex situations, our routinized responses can fall short. We are mistaken if we tell ourselves that career moves and relationship choices can be managed with our tried-and-true thinking patterns. We can't attend to the execution of our major life decisions with the same routine approach as, say, riding a bicycle.

YOUR MENTAL BLUEPRINTS CAN BE MISLEADING

In 2015, engineer and YouTube celebrity Destin Sandlin, a long-time bike rider, was given a present by a welder friend. It was a bicycle with one simple difference: Turning the handlebars to the left made the bike turn right, and vice versa. Sandlin jumped right on—no helmet required for a simple task like riding a backward bicycle!

He didn't get five feet before toppling over. He tried again and again but couldn't get any farther, his frustration growing each time. He had never thought about the assumptions that underlie his bike-riding instincts, or what the engineer in him aptly called "the algorithm that's associated with riding a bike, in your brain." Even after becoming cognizant of the disconnect between his new bike and his old algorithm, he had trouble adjusting. Whenever he wanted to adjust the bike's path, he would automatically turn the handlebars the wrong way, throwing him off the bike. "My thinking was in a rut," he said.[1]

He practiced five minutes every day for eight months. He "had many wrecks" before finally being able to ride the backward bike without falling. Even then, it took lots of concentration to override the algorithm. "It's like there's this trail in my brain, but if I wasn't paying close enough attention to it, my brain would easily lose that neural path and jump back onto the old road it was more familiar with. Any small distractions at all, like a cellphone ringing in my pocket, would instantly throw my brain back to the old control algorithm and I would wreck." He presented the bike to a wide variety of audiences, offering $200 to anyone who could ride it for ten feet. Many tried; all failed.[2]

Another term for Sandlin's brain algorithm is a mental *blueprint*. All of us carry assumptions and mental models, often implicit or unconscious, that shape how we approach decisions and take subsequent actions.[3] When our situations are stable and the context is well understood, our blueprints act as efficient shortcuts, but when we make changes in our lives or careers, we often fail to see how our blueprints don't fit. Even if we become aware of a disconnect, we still find it hard to break out of our old modes of thinking. As Sandlin pessimistically reflected on his experiences, "Once you have a rigid way of thinking in your head, sometimes you cannot change that, even if you want to."[4]

Businesspeople in arenas as disparate as startups and the corporate C-suite face this problem, and they often fall short. As a startup example, I tap Curt Schilling, who gained fame as a three-time World Series–winning pitcher and then turned to founding a startup after retiring from baseball.[5] From the C-suite, we look at Jim McNerney of General Electric and 3M.

The heights of Schilling's baseball fame came in 2004, when he was a pitcher for the Boston Red Sox. Schilling found himself pitching against his team's hated rivals, the New York Yankees, in a best-of-seven league championship series that would decide which team would move on to the World Series.

After being down 0–3, a position from which no team had ever rallied to win the league championship, the Red Sox won two games. Schilling was scheduled to pitch in game 6, but he had suffered a displaced tendon in his ankle. Determined to play, he underwent an experimental procedure in which a doctor sutured the tendon in place. Early in the game, the camera zoomed in on his foot to show blood seeping into his sock—the tendon had come loose again. Nevertheless, he persevered, allowing just one run to be scored against the Sox; that day, his team won. The Sox went on to win the league championship and the World Series. Schilling's perseverance became a baseball legend and reinforced his innate drive to become the savior in times of crisis.

What most fans didn't know about Schilling was his love of online gaming. At fourteen, Schilling received his first computer—an Apple II—and he was hooked. Within a few years, he was writing programs and participating in role-playing games nearly the entire time he was off the field. Schilling's passion continued even into his pitching career. Schilling said of his early days as a professional baseball player: "ESPN was becoming increasingly prominent, and you could go out and become the lead story on ESPN for doing nothing. I wasn't interested in jeopardizing my marriage by going out while on the road, so my computer became my outlet. I traveled with a laptop that weighed fifteen pounds."[6] As his career in baseball continued to develop, so did Schilling's penchant for games.

So when Schilling began to plan his life after baseball, he decided to pursue his lifelong passion. He was aware—but not worried—that the odds are stacked against any founder. "I had to beat the Yankees three times in nine days. I never doubted I was going to do it. My whole life was spent doing things that people didn't believe were possible. And I carried that same mentality into everything I did."[7] Here was a man used to seeing low odds of success and still winning much of the time. In addition, Schilling's baseball career brought tremendous upside: He had no trouble getting potential partners such as world-famous author R. A. Salvatore to collaborate with him. Yet his decision also had unexpected downsides.

As Schilling said, in baseball, "players play, and owners own"—no players had stakes in the ownership or profits of the business. At his company, 38 Studios (named for his uniform number), Schilling adopted the same model and maintained full ownership. His preferred CEO candidate had to threaten to walk away before Schilling finally adjusted that element of his blueprint and granted him a small amount of equity ownership, followed by equity stakes for his subsequent senior hires. Likewise, Schilling was used to working in a starting-pitching rotation of a handful of pitchers whose members all had the same job description: Each was supposed to take the ball on the day he was starting the game and pitch as deeply into the game as he could while giving up as few runs as possible. It is therefore no surprise that all four members of his early management team had similar roles, leading to destructive tensions within the group. At first Schilling also suggested that people work fourteen straight days before taking a break, as everyday baseball players often had to do. His employees forced him to adjust these expectations to more closely match their own blueprints for how to alternate work with breaks.

These disconnects started out small in the early days of 38 Studios, but the size of the breaks from reality—and their repercussions—grew along with the company, eventually proving fatal. The one and only game the company released garnered positive reviews, but sales weren't high enough to sustain the business. In 2012, 38 Studios shuttered.

It is perhaps understandable that Schilling's blueprints couldn't make the leap across such a broad gulf, from professional baseball to small-time startup. (He changed too many pillars, in Geoff Smart's terminology.) But blueprint disconnects surface even when people move between firms in the same industry. For instance, they also play a role for star equity analysts who move to new investment banks and suffer significant performance decreases lasting as long as five years.[8] For people who make more dramatic changes, the blueprint disconnects can multiply manifold, something that is often overlooked by the 23 percent of job changers who move into different segments of their industry or for the 29 percent who move into new industries altogether.[9]

Just consider the cautionary corporate tale of Jim McNerney. McNerney was in his fifties when he took over as CEO of 3M in 2001. He had been a thirty-year veteran of General Electric, working under his mentor, the legendary CEO Jack Welch, who was famed for firing 10 percent of his managers each year. McNerney had been next in line for the CEO spot at GE but was passed over for Jeff Immelt. McNerney's second-place finish didn't matter to the stock market, though. Investors were so excited about his helming 3M that the company's stock jumped a huge 20 percent the day that his selection was announced.

McNerney knew that he needed to maintain 3M's world-class innovation processes. After all, this was the company that had invented masking tape, Thinsulate, and the Post-It note. "If I dampen our enthusiasm for innovation," he said, "I've really screwed it up."[10] Yet he proceeded to do exactly that. He imported GE's celebrated Six Sigma management techniques to scrutinize processes, curb waste, and reduce defects. He streamlined 3M's operations and laid off eight thousand people. All had been elements of GE's success under Welch and had become deeply embedded in McNerney's own blueprint, but now these processes and rules constrained researchers in 3M labs. His explicit acknowledgement of the danger in harming 3M's innovation engine was not enough to change his GE-shaped blueprint. McNerney ended up leaving for Boeing, and his stint at 3M is seen as a failure in an otherwise long and successful career.

How could a star leader go so wrong? What happened to McNerney can happen to anyone. McNerney learned the hard way (and very publicly) that blueprints that worked well for us in the past can be our downfall when applied in a new arena, as they keep us from properly reacting to a different context. And this can play into habits or problem-solving techniques for any circumstance, from scheduling your time when you take a new job with a different commute to adjusting to the rhythm of having a baby in the house and still finding time to shower.

Whatever the case, it is important to bear in mind that rethinking mental blueprints requires more than a one-time fix. Sandlin observed that even after mastering—or at least becoming proficient at—the backward bicycle, he continually needed to work at counteracting his mental model. The process was long and difficult.

I have seen similar comments on a forum for travelers or emigrants who had to make the transition to driving on the "wrong" side of the road in a foreign country. One driver observed: "The level of concentration required is much higher. It was a month before I could have much of a conversation in the car and months before I turned on the radio."[11] The spouse of a traveler provided a concrete example of the dangers of "switch[ing] to auto pilot": "We were reversing out of a driveway one time and [my husband] automatically looked in the direction he would look when at home . . . and very nearly backed straight into a car coming the other way. That was a very close call!"[12]

Blueprints aren't all about how we drive (or bike) or the actions we take. On a deeper level, they can shape our values and priorities. Several years ago, while working in a finance-oriented job, Nicole realized that her professional happiness would come largely from working for a cause that was greater than herself. Of her many accomplishments, those that involved supporting others were the ones that made Nicole feel proudest. This pattern played out even in the simplest of settings. One day, she told me, after cheering on members of her track team, she remembered driving home "with my windows down and music blaring. I was perfectly happy."

Yet each time she made career decisions, she had been drawn toward only industries that pay large salaries. "We had a job board at school with hundreds of job listings around the world," she said. "Ninety percent of the time, I'd narrow the search down to the industries I had already worked in prior to school that paid well, even though I had been miserable in those jobs. The few times I would let myself scroll through different options, invariably, the relatively low salaries listed made me quickly close the browser page."

Nicole was convinced that she was not money driven. She and her husband live contentedly in a small apartment, and she drives a six-year-old Mazda. Nicole's husband is already making a substantial salary and tells her that he wants her to be able to choose a path that is aligned with a more mission-driven life. Still, the compensation issue held her back. She couldn't stop worrying that a day would come when her family would need more money than she could ever earn at one of the organizations that really appealed to her. She felt trapped in her high-paying role at a prestigious investment firm where she worked fifteen-hour days and often through the weekends.

One night, after coming home late, she asked herself: "Is this what the rest of my life is going to be like? Working on things that don't matter to me and missing out on the things that do?" Her head knew that compensation should not be the driving factor in selecting a career, but in her heart—where this particular blueprint lay—she worried about the day when money would become an issue.

Where did her mind-set come from? Only recently did Nicole recognize its roots. Having grown up in a household where her mother was the sole breadwinner, Nicole realized that she was reenacting her mother's role, foreclosing options that might prevent her from supporting a family on a single income. As she discovered, the origins of our blueprints often lurk deep in the past. In Nicole's case, as in many, her deep-seated blueprints stem from familial experiences that played out well before she could even take part in shaping her mental models. These unconscious, but highly powerful, blueprints can have devastating effects that heighten our regrets.

These influences can also affect decisions about our spouses. Psychologist Harville Hendrix says that we seek spouses who have the predominant character traits of the people who raised us—most often, our parents.[13] He had one client, John, who was dating two women: the kind, sweet Patricia and the constantly critical, emotionally unavailable Cheryl. Though Patricia was nearly perfect, John obsessed over Cheryl, especially after she told him she needed more time apart so she could date other men. John's mother was similarly distant and highly critical, often not speaking to him for several hours after he irritated her during one of her (frequent) bad moods. After one particular incident with his mother, young John ran, sobbing, to his room. He turned to face his mirror and saw himself with tears running down his face. He says he realized, in that moment, "What good is it to cry? No one cares." He wiped his tears and, remarkably, never cried again. Hendrix explains that Cheryl's coldness provoked the same unrequited longing for closeness in John, as an adult, that he had experienced as a child with his mother. The emotional power of that longing, despite its negative aspects, prevailed over his less complicated but less intense feelings for Patricia. In preferring Cheryl, John was reverting to a blueprint etched in early life.

Pause for Reflection

- Think about a time in the past when you made a major change at work or at home—in other words, you went from one set of circumstances to a very different set. What were the biggest unexpected differences between the two contexts? Were there any negative surprises that cropped up because you were not prepared for those differences?
- It is likely that there were ways in which you could have proactively identified those differences. Looking back, how might you have been able to identify them? Can you apply these strategies to a future change in context?
- Is there a particular change you know you *should* make, but can't bring yourself to do it?

Our brains, as Daniel Kahneman explains in *Thinking Fast and Slow*, are wired for complacency.[14] Faced with a difficult problem, we try to substitute a problem that's easier to solve. For small matters, such as deciding which copier to buy, the gains from decisiveness can trump the benefits of painstaking analysis. But big matters bring higher risks. We're lulled into thinking we've already conquered a challenge akin to the one that faces us when, in fact, the new issue requires a different path forward—more careful consideration of which parts of our blueprint may not apply or may even be counterproductive.

Counteracting our mental blueprints is admittedly daunting, especially once we realize that some of them are hardwired and others have been in the works since we were small. But as discussed later, *daunting* is not the same as *impossible*. Our biological and personal histories don't dictate our destinies. Habits can be changed, as long as we're willing to identify and face them. That means actively seeking out self-limiting behavior patterns, even in places where we may least expect to find them—such as in our everyday dealings with people much like ourselves.

When we head onto a new bicycle, into a new relationship, or off to take a new job, we often seek stability by involving people with whom we feel an affinity. By tapping people with whom we share similarities, we attempt to reduce the uncertainty of making a big change. Unfortunately, those similarities can heighten rather than dampen the risks we are trying to avoid.

THE DANGER OF HOMOPHILY

Think of your ten closest friends. Demographically speaking (think: race, gender, religion, socioeconomic class, and cultural background), how similar are they to you? If you're like most people, your friends are probably far more like you than not. This is because birds of a feather tend to flock together, a tendency academics call *homophily*, which simply means an affinity for similar others. Homophily in race and ethnicity are often the strongest barriers to social diversity in our lives, followed by age, religion, education, occupation, and gender.[15] Not only is it difficult to create diversity among our social relationships; it's even harder to maintain it: Ties between nonsimilar individuals dissolve at a higher rate than those between people who are alike.[16]

At the most basic level, geographic proximity draws people together. A study of the Dyckman Housing Projects in Manhattan found that 88 percent of apartment dwellers' closest friends lived in the same building, and almost half were on the same floor.[17] Race and age were also powerful predictors of friendship: 60 percent of people listed as friends were in the same age category as the respondent, and 72 percent of all reported friends were of the same race. Friendships among people of different ages and races were found almost exclusively among residents who lived very close to one another.

Homophily also has powerful effects on our political interactions. In the 1972 presidential election, Richard Nixon beat George McGovern in a landslide, winning forty-nine of fifty states and more than 60 percent of the popular vote. In the aftermath of the election, Pauline Kael of the *New Yorker* famously commented: "I live in a rather special world. I only know one person who voted for Nixon. Where they are I don't know. They're outside my ken. But sometimes when I'm in a theater I can feel them."[18] (This is sometimes apocryphally quoted as, "How could Nixon have won? Nobody I know voted for him!")

Kael is not the only one who succumbs to the temptation to flock to birds of a similar political feather. A consortium of thirty-nine universities collaborated to study a representative sample of 64,600 American voters in the 2016 election.[19] They found that about 63 percent of Clinton voters talked only with other Clinton voters, and another 12 percent talked only with Clinton voters and undecideds. Similarly, about 69 percent of Trump voters talked only with other Trump voters, and another 8 percent talked only with Trump voters and undecideds. In short, say two of the researchers from the study, "Seventy-five percent of Clinton voters do not have a single Trump supporter in their immediate network, and just the reverse is true for Trump voters."[20] Sometimes we even go out of our way to shut down interactions with those whose political feather differs from ours. For instance, a 2014 Pew study found that on Facebook, 31 percent of consistent conservatives and 44 percent of consistent liberals had muted or unfriended someone because of political disagreements.[21]

Even where rules of thumb suggest that homophily won't be as prevalent, it still is. When it comes to romantic relationships, we often believe that opposites attract. However, recent research on 231,707 people found strong personality homophily among both romantic partners and friends.[22] Research on homogamy (marrying a like partner) also shows that spouses tend to match in a variety of social and demographic areas, such as education, race, religion, occupation, and family socioeconomic background. Researchers Debra Blackwell and Daniel Lichter analyzed a sample of 10,847 women in the United States, ages fifteen to forty-four. They found that dating, cohabiting, and married couples tend to pair homophilously with respect to education, race, and religion. Individuals with less than a high school degree were 52 times more likely to marry a similarly educated person than someone possessing more education than themselves. Catholics were 6 times more likely to marry Catholics, while faiths marked "Other" (non-Christian) were *65 times* more likely to marry someone who also marked their faith as "Other" (excluding those who marked themselves as having no religious affiliation). Homogamy by race was exceptionally strong, with African Americans 110 times more likely to marry African Americans and with Caucasians 5 times more likely to have a Caucasian spouse.[23]

In business we tend to assume that performance drives decisions, especially given the accepted wisdom that companies perform better if they create diverse teams that are poised to handle diverse tasks. Indeed, when the American sociologist Howard Aldrich and his colleagues studied small businesses, they expected to find an entrepreneurial environment in which functional diversity ruled, with teams including a "build" person who creates the product and a "sell" person who gets it into customers' hands. Instead, they found homophily to be almost the rule, with companies more likely to have "build" or "sell" people but not both. They also found that gender uniformity was five times more likely to occur than they expected—and racial homophily was an incredible forty-six times more likely.[24] Only entrepreneurs who are particularly vigilant about homophily are able to counter such strong tendencies.

Teams stacked with like people hide major risks. On top of their lack of diversity in skills and knowledge, homophilous colleagues tend to say yes when a no might be more appropriate. Say you're a product designer who has teamed up with another designer. "Let me show you my ideal product!" he exclaims. Instead of pushing back on his design by pointing out that it will be impossible to sell the product to customers, you give your colleague a thumbs-up that a salesperson never would have given him. Or you're a member of a two-salesperson team. Instead of pointing out that your colleague's ideal product may be technically unfeasible, as would a technical partner, you reinforce the product concept. And it's easy to see how a like-team's smaller network of social and business contacts limits the information they receive. Imagine, for example, that you've been working for years in law firm recruiting but think that you might enjoy a human resources role more, as was the case with one of my executive MBA students. She might ask a mentor for help in figuring out whether to move into human resources. However, if the mentor is too similar in background and outlook, their combined perspectives may turn out to be too narrow to identify all the factors that would be critical to making a successful move. Or let's say you're seeking a new hire for your department or a new corporate partner for your company. If the only people you contact are those whose networks are similar to yours, you'll have a very limited choice of candidates or partners.

Vivek Khuller, the founder of the electronic-ticketing startup Smartix, was a native of India who had been an engineer before going to business school. Even though he had no experience in the ticketing industry or its venues, he told me, he saw a big opportunity to replace paper tickets with electronic ones.

He initially considered a wide variety of potential cofounders, including someone with a background in private equity who could help raise money for the startup, and another person whose family owned a prominent sports venue and who had deep knowledge of the industry. Yet he was most attracted to a cofounder who was also a native of India, a former engineer, and did not know anything about ticketing or venues despite his overall brilliance. He disregarded the other candidates and focused on attracting the like-minded cofounder.

This resulted in duplicated strengths and magnified weaknesses, a very common result of homophily. The team had an overdose of engineering thinking combined with ignorance of how a venue operates and how a venue operator makes buying decisions. A year later, the company shut down, only to have StubHub fill the void and eventually be bought by eBay for $310 million. A friend of the founder sent him the press release about StubHub's sale, with a note: "This could have been you." (With friends like that, who needs enemies?)

When we discuss Khuller's decisions in my course, the students quickly see how homophily left gaping holes in that team. Yet many insist that they would be able to avoid the same pitfall. Are they right?

Without telling them, I test their susceptibility to homophily in the context of the small study teams in which they prepare for each class session. At the beginning of the semester, I assign them to diverse teams of the type that Howard Aldrich expected to find—one engineering student, one business student, and one from neither program. Later I disband these teams and tell the students to form their own groups. After they critique Khuller's homophily, I put up a slide showing, side by side, the composition of their original assigned study teams and their self-formed teams. The comparison is striking. The self-formed teams epitomize homophily, with many all-engineer and all-business groupings.

Nervous laughs spread across the room as the students realize how susceptible they are (and will be) to this powerful pull. When they reflect on their experiences in their self-formed teams, they realize that succumbing to homophily hindered their study teams' effectiveness by leading them to miss key aspects. The all-engineering teams often neglect the market's view of the product being produced, and the all-business teams underestimate the operational challenges of developing the product.

Another risk of homophily is that it often fosters assumptions about consensus. "We see eye to eye on the basics," the thinking goes, "so there's no need to formalize our agreement." The cofounders of photo-sharing app Snapchat were peas in a pod—college fraternity brothers with similar strengths. They relied on only a vague oral "founder agreement"; as close friends, they didn't see the need for a legal document. Soon their homophily began to cause problems, though. Their skill sets overlapped. CEO Evan Spiegel felt that cofounder and CMO Reggie Brown added no value and that he could do the marketing job himself. He ended up firing Brown and locking him out of the company's systems. Brown had assumed that the equity would be split equally, but Spiegel essentially pretended that Brown's founding share didn't exist.[25]

The damage to the relationship was substantial. "Do not forget that these were fraternity brothers . . . they were best friends," said Brown's attorney, Luan Tran. When Snapchat started, "the last thing on their mind was sitting down and lawyering up."[26] Brown kept tabs on Snapchat's progress even after he was booted. After hearing that the company received a $3 billion takeover offer from Facebook, Brown immediately sued Snapchat for what he believed to be his rightful share of the company. Eventually, he received $157.5 million to settle the lawsuit, though in disclosing the sum, the company went out of its way not to name Brown or refer to him as a cofounder.[27]

Not only does homophily sometimes lull people into ignoring the need for explicit agreements; it also skews decision making in other ways. Economist Paul Gompers and his colleagues looked at 3,510 individual venture capitalists who invested in 11,895 portfolio companies from 1975 to 2003, focusing on the deals where multiple venture capitalists invested together in a round of financing, also known as *syndication*. They analyzed how similar those syndicating venture capitalists were in their "ability-based" characteristics, such as both having a degree from a top university, and "affinity-based" characteristics, such as a shared ethnicity. They found a great deal of affinity-based homophily: The probability that two venture capitalists would syndicate together increased by 22.8 percent if they were part of the same ethnic minority group. They found similar effects for other affinity-based characteristics, such as having attended the same school as undergraduates or having worked previously at the same company.[28]

Those homophilous collaborations significantly harmed the venture capitalists' performance as investors. Gompers and his authors state, "Collaboration with someone from the same ethnic minority group comes at the expense of a 20% reduction in performance."[29] The more alike the two investors were regarding their affinity-based characteristics, the more likely their investment performance suffered, often dramatically so. (In contrast, collaborating for ability-based characteristics increased investment performance.) The researchers suggest a possible reason for the finding: "Individuals may lower the expected-return hurdle and due-diligence standards on a project for the opportunity to work with similar others because they derive personal utility from the collaboration."[30] The short-term intangible returns of homophily compromised the long-term financial returns venture capitalists are supposed to prioritize, a sterling example of the "easy" decision that becomes harmful in the long run.

Indeed, homophilous collaborations are much easier to assemble. Searching for individuals with diverse talents and contacts often poses a major challenge. Most of us would have to reach far beyond our social and business networks to find highly qualified individuals with complementary capabilities.

In organizations, homophily is reinforced and perpetuated by the popular yet ill-defined concept of cultural fit. It's a go-to phrase among hiring managers. A Cubiks International survey found that more than 80 percent of employers worldwide named cultural fit a top hiring priority.[31] The same holds for the personal interests of job candidates. In a study of professionals involved in hiring at top-tier firms in law, finance, and consulting, Lauren Rivera of Northwestern University found that interviewers were primarily interested in candidates whose hobbies, hometowns, and biographies matched their own. For example, while an African American attorney responded favorably to a fictional Hispanic candidate's upbringing in a rough neighborhood and experience with Teach for America, noting that they would have something they could "really talk about," a Caucasian male banker found the same candidate to be lackluster, saying that "these types of extracurriculars like volunteering and tutoring seem sort of canned as opposed to something like watching sports or something that shows this is a real person." An attorney Rivera interviewed said of potential hires: "You think, 'Is this someone I want to hang out with? Just someone who I'd rather go and get a beer with after work?' . . . You have to be excited about them."[32]

Too often, interviewers rationalize a hire as being a good cultural fit when they want to hire someone but can't point to the concrete value that the person would add. Geoff Smart of the G. H. Smart hiring consultancy has seen firsthand the problems with hiring for cultural fit. As he explained to my class: "A lot of interviewers make the mistake of trying to figure out early on, 'Do I have chemistry with this candidate?' But you could have chemistry with a lot of people, so the more limiting constraint is whether someone's likely to perform well or not. Job performance and chemistry are not related!"

Even if you design a team that is the ultimate in diversity and is eager to raise alternative perspectives, chances are its diversity will soon wane. Unless groups add new members, they tend to become more homogeneous over time. Association with a group reinforces shared tastes and discourages divergent ones,[33] and atypical members leave the organization sooner than typical members.[34] Furthermore, in a series of studies, Elizabeth Umphress and her colleagues found that high-status incumbents in a traditional hierarchical environment prefer to interact with each other, leaving low-status new members to rely on one another as they attempt to integrate within the organization.[35] Employers who hire a diverse array of employees still have little say in how employees spend time together at breaks or after work. Despite the employer's best intentions, informal cliques often arise along racial, socioeconomic, or gender lines, limiting knowledge sharing across the company.

Pause for Reflection

- Imagine that you were to tap your five closest friends to work on a collaborative project with you.

  - Would there be holes in the team's skills, the networks it could tap, or its diversity of perspectives?

  - Are the team members' races or ethnic backgrounds, their educational experiences, their religions, and their economic statuses similar to yours? If so, might these similarities work against you when you need to complete substantive projects, or are they more likely to become a strength?

- Now imagine a team where everyone differs in skills, networks, and perspectives. What benefits and challenges would such a team pose for you in terms of achieving the team's or your goals?

CHAPTER 6

REDRAW YOUR BLUEPRINT AND
RETHINK YOUR ROUTINES

IN CHAPTERS 2 AND 4, we see how some of the most experienced founders avoid both inertia and impulsivity, as well as how they overcome a fear of
failure and learn to plan for success. In this chapter, we look at two more attributes: avoiding overreliance on mental blueprints and resisting the powerful
tendency to flock to similar others.

The skills covered in previous chapters are important ones, but they are also
fairly attainable. Think of them as good habits that our founders were adept at
learning to advance their unconventional ideas at reasonable speed, allowing
them to look ahead without looking down. By contrast, this chapter asks us to
dig deeper and stretch further. Blueprints and homophily are so ingrained in
our minds, so organic to our thinking, that most of us don't even see them. We
typically don't identify them as potentially problematic, much less try to resist
them. How do successful entrepreneurs achieve the perspective needed to question such deep-seated notions?

BATTLE THE BLUEPRINT

Failure is an excellent teacher. Would-be entrepreneurs typically try out a lot
of quasi-formed ideas, sometimes even in childhood, and their failures uncover holes in their preformed beliefs. Jalapeño lemonade turns out not to be
an immediate hit on a summer day. Styrofoam turns out not to be durable
boat-building material. An app for identifying insects turns out to be much

too complicated. While some people come to doubt *themselves* in the face of such failures, successful founders have a different reaction: They begin to doubt their *assumptions*.

Unlike self-doubt, which undermines motivation, doubting entrenched convictions can be intensely exciting, even if it doesn't feel that way at first. It can lead you to see connections and opportunities that others have overlooked. Assumption questioning is especially beneficial at both life and career inflection points, which is where mental blueprints can pose the biggest threat. To cultivate a healthy sense of doubt, you can learn to proactively probe for blind spots and demand pushback from others to help identify overlooked holes. Let's look at each of these strategies in detail and how to patch holes once you find them.

Proactively Probe for Blind Spots

I've often seen entrepreneurs, whether early in a new venture or even before embarking on it, explicitly break down their startup plans and compare them against the assumptions that constitute the blueprints they have accumulated from their prior personal and professional experiences. They focus on three key areas, which I call the Three Rs: the prior *relationships* they tap to find cofounders and key hires, how they make decisions and allocate *roles*, and how they divide the *rewards* and other incentives to attract and motivate the right people.

Curt Schilling, the World Series–winning pitcher and online-game entrepreneur discussed in Chapter 5, made mistakes in all three areas. He initially tapped the relationships he had developed with his online gaming friends by hiring them as his first employees and then had to undo those hires in favor of more-professional employees. The roles within Schilling's early management team were very similar to each other, akin to the pitching rotations to which he had belonged. From the resulting tensions, he learned to create distinctive roles within his leadership team and to adjust the team's composition accordingly. He also had to change his baseball-driven "owners own" blueprint, adopting a "key contributors own a stake" approach that's a far more productive approach to rewards within startups. Schilling was a quick learner, but even he wasn't able to adjust until after his blueprints had caused heightened tensions, turnover, and growth challenges. Such blind spots could have been surfaced a lot earlier by proactive probing rather than reactive fixing.

A job change is one of the inflection points where probing for holes in our blueprints can have a big impact, as researchers Boris Groysberg and Robin Abrahams found in a study of four hundred executive-search consultants from more than fifty industries.[1] Their research underscores the importance of questioning assumptions related to all Three Rs when contemplating a career move: for example, that the people in the new environment will be helpful and compatible (relationships), that the position will match the official job title and description (roles), and that the employer is financially stable and will be able to maintain a strong market position (a factor affecting the potential rewards).

Groysberg and Abrahams found that the most successful job switchers examine the new landscape, breaking down their blueprints to see which parts will apply and which won't. They ask, "What if I'm wrong about this position? What is the evidence that this company would be good for me?" Then they adjust the outdated elements. A key piece of the findings is the importance of probing and persistence—of continuing to ask these questions at every stage, despite the effects of high-pressure recruitment. How can we follow this guidance and avoid being lulled into passivity?

Create Reminders and Checkpoints

When students or new founders enroll in my course or my Founder Bootcamp, the first thing they do is complete a self-assessment of what decisions they would make at sixteen key forks in the road that my research has shown are particularly important for founders. For instance, would they solo-found or find cofounders? Would they keep strong control of decision making or share decisions? Would they prefer to avoid taking outside financing or attract investors? Their initial results capture their instincts about each option— their heart-driven choices. After we delve into each of these decisions—after they've thought clearly about each decision and learned to make head-driven choices—I have them take the same sixteen-question assessment again, afterward highlighting which of their decisions have changed. On average, about five of the participants' sixteen decisions get reversed.

Yet time after time I have seen that simply gaining awareness of these disconnects is not enough. It is too easy to continue on autopilot, following your heart instead of pulling back on the reins when facing a decision where head and heart diverge. Instead, the best founders find concrete ways to remind themselves to think twice when they hit a decision point where a blueprint disconnect exists. The most impactful solution I have seen? A founder who posted his sixteen-question results above his desk with the disconnects highlighted. He developed a habit of looking at the sheet whenever he was facing an important decision to see whether it related to his disconnects.

Figure 3 is a sixteen-decision map in which a student could see clearly what her head was telling her to do at each fork in the road after we had studied each decision in depth (the italicized item in each row of the table) and which answers differed from what her heart had been telling her to do prior to the semester (the arrows pointing from her original answer to a new answer). For ten of the decisions, head and heart were in sync, so she could default to what felt right. For the six other decisions (the ones with gray backgrounds), head and heart diverged. Studying those six decisions sparked the realization that she should avoid choices that imperiled her control of the startup, especially when involving investors and grappling with succession issues. She printed out this map and began developing the habit of looking at it before making any of the sixteen decisions to see if she was facing one of the six forks in the road. She also learned to be particularly vigilant at the stage in which she might involve outside investors, where half of her changes occurred. The decision map underscored the need for her to be continually mindful of how her tendencies conflicted with her real goals.

Remember the problem of adjusting to driving on the other side of the road? Even drivers who were conscious of the need to change would lapse back into autopilot, making moves that would have been perfectly sensible in their home countries but were life threatening in their new locales. This was particularly likely when they were tired and couldn't devote their energy and attention to battling their blueprints. Just as my founder had posted his "disconnects" map, the other-side-of-the-road drivers in Chapter 5 include one who battled autopilot by setting up visual and active reminders of the difference in context: "I actually think driving a stick is better. . . . W[ith] an automatic things can feel too normal/just like back home, and one can drift into sort of 'auto pilot mode'. That is when you get into trouble. The [sight of the] gear lever sitting over [there] on your left side and having to shift is just another mental cue that things are different. Helps keep one alert."[2]

If you can't change the situation or your setting to incorporate prominent reminders, try changing the rhythm of your process. For instance, creating times when you review progress toward goals can help mitigate the negative impact of speeding ahead. Another founder who took the sixteen-question assessment set calendar reminders for himself so that he could prepare for decisions that required deviating from his blueprints. The decisions weren't necessarily mapped out, but the thoughtful pauses were.

Connie Gersick of UCLA found that, at venture capital–backed startups, checkpoints—usually established by the passage of a certain amount of time or the expenditure of a certain amount of capital—trigger healthy and proactive change because they enable leaders to ascertain whether a coveted goal is likely to be reached. At a medical-products company Gersick studied called M-Tech, CEO Charles Powers was confident about their promising new product. To evaluate their progress and facilitate planning, the CEO had adopted a policy of having key meetings every six months. He treated each year as two halves with a midyear checkpoint to assess progress. Six months provided enough time to implement plans and gather data on how they were performing, while allowing for course correction at those checkpoints. Regarding their new product, the CEO said, "We had sold aggressively, with a salesforce in place by January." However, in July at the CEO's regular midyear check-in with the vice president of R&D, they realized that the market just wasn't there. The company swiftly changed course and backed what had been considered its second-best product, which turned out to be a success. Both the CEO and the investor perceived this decision as having saved the company.[3]

While firefighters aren't often compared to entrepreneurs, they are another group expected to make high-stakes decisions with limited information and time. They use checkpoints too. Researchers investigating urban fire ground commanders noted that experienced commanders make decisions "without conscious deliberation between option alternatives."[4] Instead, they have a large bank of prior experiences—essentially, accumulated blueprints—on which they draw, and to which they compare their new situations. Also like founders, veteran commanders build in checkpoints to ensure that if the situation doesn't play out in a way that's similar to past experience, they can catch the error in judgment and change course. For instance, the researchers found that when an experienced commander arrived at the scene of a building fire, he would watch the rate of spread momentarily to test if he was correct in his initial assumption about the combustibility of the fuel source. What he observed would determine his next instructions to his team.

Checkpoints require you to assess the changing landscape around you. By forcing reflection, they can help you integrate new information about whether your goal is now more or less likely to happen, enabling you to course-correct as needed. Many areas of life can benefit from such "checkpoint thinking." For instance, one of my students who was engaged to be married decided that when she became a first-time parent, she and her future spouse should set monthly checkpoints to assess the effect on their relationship. At those monthly discussions, they would see whether they needed to adjust elements of their prebaby

Potential participants in the startup	Decision area	Decisions oriented toward maintaining control	Decisions oriented toward maximizing wealth
Cofounders	Solo versus team	Remain solo founder	*Build cofounding team*
	Relationships	Tap immediate circle of friends and family to find cofounders	*Tap both strong and weak/distant ties to find cofounders*
	Roles	*Keep strong control of decision making* ←	Share decision making with cofounder
	Rewards	Maintain most or all equity ownership	*Share equity to attract and/ or motivate cofounders or critical hires*
Hires	Relationships	*Hire within close personal network (friends, family, and others) as required*	Aggressively tap broader network (unfamiliar candidates) to find best hires
	Roles	Keep control of important decisions	*Delegate important decision making to appropriate expert*
	Rewards	*Hire less expensive "rising star" (potentially up-and-coming) junior employees*	Hire more expensive, experienced "rock star" employees
Investors	Self-fund versus take outside capital	*Self-fund; bootstrap* ←	Take outside capital
	Sources of capital	*Raise capital from friends and family or money-only angels* ←	Target experienced angels or venture capitalists
	Terms	*Resist terms (e.g., supermajority rights) that threaten control*	Be open to terms necessary to attract best investors (e.g., giving them supermajority rights)
	Board of directors	*Avoid building official board or build board I can control* ←	Get best investors and directors even if it might imperil board control
Successors	Openness to succession	*Resist giving up the CEO position* ←	Be open to giving up CEO position if the next stage of growth might be beyond my capabilities
	Desired role after succession	*Leave the company after being replaced as founder-CEO* ←	Move into a non-CEO role (one that is aligned with my interests) in the company after being replaced as founder-CEO

Potential participants in the startup	Decision area	Decisions oriented toward maintaining control	Decisions oriented toward maximizing wealth
Other factors	Preferred rate of startup growth	Gradual to moderate	Fast to explosive
	Career dilemma: when to found	Wait until I am well equipped with skills and experience to launch and build startup without much help	Allow important gaps that should be filled by involving others
	Size of pie versus slice of pie	Found a venture worth $5 million, of which I own 100%	Found a venture worth $100 million, of which I own 5%
Most likely outcome		Maintain control; build less value	Build financial value; imperil control

FIGURE 3. Sixteen-question map
Note: Gray shading indicates head-versus-heart decisions.

blueprint to better fit their new situation. Questions she anticipated addressing at each checkpoint included: Were we able to spend enough time together this month? Is either of us feeling disconnected, lonely, or stressed? Have we been fulfilling our promise of weekly date nights? Given these assessments, how should we adjust our parenting and spousal approach before things get too sour?

Similarly, you can make a point of checking in with yourself regularly about any endeavor you've undertaken, not only to measure your progress but also to question your assumptions. That book you're writing about biodegradable packaging, for example: You've been at it for a year, and you've turned out some scintillating prose, but should you reexamine your assumption that a book is the best way to effect change? Would you be more effective organizing a non-profit educational organization or a panel at a green conference? Or would it be better to look for a job as the sustainability officer in a local corporation?

While self-diagnosis is a start, it often isn't enough to break us free from our blueprints. It's just too easy to lapse into old assumptions unless we summon targeted sources of pushback or deputize others to help us.

Demand Pushback from Others

Curt Schilling's model of not giving ownership stakes to employees and maintaining a baseball-like vacation policy didn't change until his preferred CEO candidate pushed back against his blueprint. Other entrepreneurs find that an even better plan is to give hires explicit permission—even a mandate—to push back on their ideas and practices. In fact, founders often recruit colleagues or advisors with greater experience—and more-relevant blueprints—to question their decisions.

Having been a long-time executive at telecommunications giant GTE, Barry Nalls could have had several devastating disconnects between the deep big-company blueprint he had developed at GTE over more than two decades and the demands of founding telecom-services company Masergy. As he took on the role of founder, Nalls had a nagging feeling that he had holes in his blueprint. An early sign of trouble showed in simply reading numbers:

> The most difficult change—this sounds small, but it really wasn't—came when I would look at numbers. At GTE, I would automatically add three zeros or six zeros to every number I would look at. You see "15," that means 15,000 or 15,000,000, not 15. In the early phases of Masergy, looking at how much we were spending, I'd say, "We couldn't be spending $15,000 for that!" They'd tell me, "Nope, it's $15." It took me quite a while to make small numbers relevant. I spent 25 years looking at numbers in the millions. I had to struggle to change that.[5]

So Nalls sought ways to identify and fill his holes.

Most centrally, Nalls sensed that he was unprepared to deal with the funding landscape for his startup. He reached out to an ex-employee who was now a junior partner at a venture capital firm. Nalls asked him to review the draft of his pitch: "He threw it right back at me: 'You can't give this detailed a plan to a VC! VCs want to know you're thinking about all those details, but they want to see major milestones. Just give me three milestones, not a task list with hundreds of things! Tell me something big I can look forward to on a specific date that shows me the investment was used wisely.'"[6] The GTE practice of providing point-by-point specifics would not have flown.

At the same time, Nalls's contact said he hadn't included enough detail about the team itself. Nalls had led his presentation with a description of his strategy, but investors would insist on hearing first about his personal background, something for which he had not created a single slide. Nalls learned that "VCs believe you can take a bad business plan and put it in the hands of good management, and they'll make something of it. But a good plan in bad hands will fail every time."[7]

Nalls began to see the specific ways in which his long-time GTE experience tracked him one way when he needed to go another, with his pitch deck being a microcosm of the adjustments he needed to make. While GTE senior executives wanted to see that you had thought through every detail, VCs knew that even the most thought-through startup plans would have to change and that the key was to focus on a small number of high priorities. At GTE, the company name itself sold new business, and individual bios were irrelevant. In unproven startups, key people are front and center.

Nalls was able to take this expert advice and add three to four pages on himself and three to four pages on the people who were going to join him. He did the hard thinking necessary to zoom in on the three most important milestones he would have to hit, and he replaced his detailed task plan with a much simpler one. Adjusting his blueprint paid off: When he pitched to investors, his presentation rang true. Nalls raised $3 million in venture capital funding and was able to attract the top partners from key firms to sit on his board.[8]

To get help assessing your own blueprint disconnects, consider who is on your personal board of directors. Have any of these people had experience in your new context? If they have, great. If not, consider: Who understands you and your blueprint, and the demands of where you are heading, so they can highlight for you the biggest potential danger areas? Find a favorite professor or former boss with whom you've stayed in touch and chat about key inflection points you're facing. Call on your uncle or aunt who was successful in your favorite new extracurricular activity or the industry in which you're starting to work. If you're contemplating a transition to marriage or parenthood, tap someone whose family life you admire and who can be counted on for candid advice. Do you enjoy spending time with his kids, and are you impressed with how the children interact with each other and with their parents? To what do those parents (and maybe even those kids) attribute those successes? If you're thinking of relocating to a new city, going back to school, or switching fields, find a friend of a friend who has been there and done that. In retrospect, what decisions and actions does she now consider to have been the most important ingredients in her transition?

In a work setting, you might deputize a colleague or your boss by periodically asking for feedback, especially as you're acclimating to your new context and could use extra input to understand your holes. At the end of your first few weeks, ask your manager if there's anything she'd like you to do differently or for areas on which you should focus more. Each time you do so, if you get one item in each of the three categories of Start, Stop, and Keep, you will accelerate your adjustment considerably. (It might feel unnatural, but you can try a similar process at home, to accelerate your development as a spouse!) Don't get lured into thinking that managers will tell you this proactively; they often will not. This makes it even more important for you to play the powerful "I'm new here; can you help me?" card. But bear in mind that this strategy isn't just for people who are starting out. If you've been someplace for a long time, you've surely developed a blueprint. Demanding pushback can help you shake up your blueprint or explore whether you are stuck in a rut. Recall from Chapter 4 the student-paper exhortation I put up on my office wall: "It's easy to get stuck in a rut, especially if you're good at what you do." Instead, take ownership of the need to probe your own disconnects.

Then be sure to actually *listen to* and act on the critique you've encouraged. Even if the head understands that we can benefit from heightening differences rather than smoothing them over, to the heart it can be "terribly painful" to raise and work through differences, says management professor Leslie Perlow of Harvard Business School: "Most people decide it's easier to cover up their differences than to try to discuss them."[9] They feel that remaining silent will be a better way to get their work done and to maintain relationships. Later, as their resentment grows, they discover that both their work and their relationships are suffering. Nicole, the finance professional described in Chapter 5 as struggling to find a better career fit, admitted to me that for a long time she ignored the opinions of outside advisors. It wasn't until she realized how miserable she had become—"working long hours for something that didn't matter to me at all"—that she finally began to listen. At that point, "life wouldn't let me ignore what my mentors were telling me."

Emulate successful founders by absorbing constructive dissent without giving in to despair. An idealistic young man considering seminary school scheduled a chat with an older acquaintance who had chaired many clergy-search committees for his faith community. Their frank discussion of the sometimes-brutal politics of boards and congregations armed the would-be seminarian with valuable insight into his career options—but didn't derail his aspirations.

Successful founders' ability to hear unsettling advice without surrendering to disappointment is related to their tendency, mentioned at the beginning of this chapter, to doubt only their assumptions, not themselves, when they hit setbacks. This is despite the intensely personal nature of entrepreneurship that Barry Nalls discovered. Venture capitalists may see founders' individual competencies as crucial, but successful entrepreneurs find ways to think of themselves as distinct from their ideas. They know that a great entrepreneur can—and will—have bad ideas as well as good ones. This capacity for putting negative information into perspective speaks to another important founder quality: flexibility.

Develop Blueprint Flexibility

Some blueprints are incredibly hard to adjust once they have solidified. Exhibit A: the eight months it took Destin Sandlin to ride the backward bike and, even after that, the intense concentration required to keep riding it successfully.

Psychologists have highlighted the importance of developing psychological flexibility—for example, the ability to shift between multiple coping mechanisms depending on the situation—rather than adhering to the strategy with which we feel most comfortable.[10] For instance, say psychologists Todd Kashdan of George Mason University and Jonathan Rottenberg of the University of South Florida: "An organized, conscientious person will tend to be responsible and restrained across most situations. However, this person's dominant response becomes problematic if the situation actually calls for bold action (e.g., a diner at an adjacent table appears to be choking)."[11]

In many instances, counteracting our dominant response requires a top-down strategy of tuning into the demands of a situation, vetoing our initial impulse to do nothing or to respond stereotypically, and deciding on a risky course of action (all, we hope, before the diner at the adjacent table succumbs). The challenge is compounded by our tendency to not notice that a situation calls for unaccustomed action—or even that a "situation" has arisen. In a classic experiment, participants were shown a video of basketball players and asked to count the number of times they passed the ball. For five seconds in the middle of the video, a man in a gorilla suit walks to center court, turns to the camera, pounds his chest, and walks off. A stunning 73 percent of the people failed to notice the gorilla as they focused on the counting task to which they had become accustomed.[12]

Similarly, it is important to develop blueprint flexibility: the ability to shift your mind-set and behaviors depending on the situation at hand. If you have developed only a single, deeply ingrained blueprint, this is quite hard. In your career, you may face this challenge if you have worked for only one company (or taught at one university, as was my case until I taught as a visiting professor at three others). You may also face it if you have lived in only one city (as is true of three of my children, who have lived in the same house in Boston all of their lives). If you fit this mold, you can enhance your flexibility by going to work for another company or taking time to experience another city.

Barry Nalls had worked at GTE for two decades when he decided to explore becoming a founder. Had he worked at even two companies, instead of just the one, his blueprint would not have been as rigid and monolithic. He realized that he had not seen the inside of anything smaller than GTE, so he decided to work for startups before breaking out on his own. He ran marketing and product strategy for one and then led technical strategy for another. Doing so enabled him to develop a wider range of blueprint elements and to identify as many disconnects as possible before he became a founder.

The startups challenged his well-worn, big-company thinking patterns—his reliance on gradual process, his belief that every employee needs a niche and that every niche needs an employee, his expectation that colleagues would step forward to guide him if he veered off course. He learned the value of making quick decisions and being a jack-of-all-trades, and he recognized that in many instances he would have sole responsibility for keeping himself on track.

It could be argued that moving to a radically different context, as Nalls did, establishes new thought patterns that quickly become ingrained. But this wasn't true for Destin Sandlin and his bicycle blueprints, and it wasn't true for Nalls, whose accumulation of blueprints from his small-business upbringing, his large-company work, and his startup-hire experiences enhanced his flexibility as a founder. And even if a new blueprint overshadows an old one, the process of grappling with competing blueprints helps us better identify and question our assumptions—such as that the people who are most similar to us are among the smartest, most competent individuals in the world.

FIGHT THE NEED TO FLOCK TOGETHER

At the business school of the University of Southern California, the dean's office arranges lunches between duos of departments, often ones that otherwise would not mix, and provides a free lunch to any faculty members who show up to meet and chat. I have participated in sessions like those, and they're memorable—at the most recent one, I got to learn about a department chair's unexpected interest in the science of elevators.

It's striking, when you think about it, that a prominent university in the midst of a great crossroads—Los Angeles is the second-largest metropolis in the United States and one of the major cities of the Pacific Rim—finds it necessary to institute a formal program to entice faculty members out of their small, accustomed circles. But that's a reflection of human nature: Even in such a cosmopolitan place, homophily is an almost irresistible force.

What's more striking is how many of the most successful entrepreneurs manage to counteract this force. On their own or with help, they come to perceive the disadvantages of homophily and take action to surround themselves with diverse viewpoints.

In 1998, Tony Tjan, now the CEO of the venture capital firm the Cue Ball Group, was a recent MBA graduate with strengths in architecting ideas, vision, and strategy. He wanted to start an internet-services consulting company and was looking for a cofounder. There was one candidate that he certainly did not want to consider, a section mate with whom he was assigned to take every class during his first year in business school. "I had a really negative—even visceral—reaction to him in class," Tjan explained to my class, "because everything turned into an operations discussion. You're in Strategy class? He'd talk about operations or process every time. Marketing? He'd say, 'Well, the reason this company succeeded was due to its marketing process. . . .' He had this squeaky voice. I wanted to kill the guy!"

However, Tjan's friends and advisors pushed him to reconsider because his section mate's operations talents were a perfect complement to Tjan's strengths. He did so and gained an appreciation for the danger of succumbing to the cognitive bias to look for those with whom we are most comfortable. He told me, "Thank God I listened because he turned out to be the perfect person for the team." Once he learned to look beyond his visceral reaction, Tjan realized, "As a person, he had a goodness of character that was rare. His values and commitment were irreproachable." In the end, Tjan and his partner raised more than $100 million in capital for their firm, ZEFER, before it was acquired.

How do entrepreneurs manage to avoid the homophily trap, and how can we follow suit? A good place to start is by adopting a set of two simple complementary solutions.

Adopt Checklists and Check-Ins

Tim Westergren experienced years of frustration as a musician, unable to find a loyal audience for his music: "It was great artistically, but very discouraging professionally, driving a van all over the West Coast for years, crashing in friends' basements and never getting noticed. It was a lot of years with little to show for it." Tim found himself wondering: When a new album came out, how could musicians find fans whose tastes might be a good match for the album? How could fans discover new music of which they might not otherwise be aware? Westergren began to form an idea that eventually turned into his Music Genome Project: "I had gotten really accustomed to thinking of music tastes as a set of attributes; a film director would share songs with me that he liked, I would break down those songs into a set of attributes, and I had to go back to the studio and translate that into a composition with similar attributes. I wanted to 'bottle' that process that was going on in my head into a software product that could come up with intelligent recommendations of other kinds of music that someone might like." He decided to found a company that would use technology to build a "music genome" to connect fans with music that matched their tastes.[13]

A natural inclination at this point might be for Westergren to tap other musicians to help him—to chat with friends, find a few who were passionate about the idea, and form a team. Indeed, many founders succumb to that inclination. But such a team would come with many of the challenges we've seen, such as redundancies in skills and gaping holes. For instance, who among these musician cofounders would be able to develop the technology or build the company's operations?

Westergren resisted that inclination and instead built a team that hit on all three key areas necessary for building this online music company: The online part would require a technical whiz, the music element would require musical and music-industry expertise, and the company aspect would require a CEO with a business background. Checking off the music-expert box was easy—it was Westergren himself. Next, he leveraged "the strength of weak ties" by tapping his extended network rather than relying on the stronger, closer ties that are often the first contacts we think to tap but that pose a greater risk of homophily.[14] For the CEO box, Westergren used his extended network to find Jon Kraft, the husband of a friend of Westergren's wife. Kraft had been founder and CEO of a startup that had been backed by a prominent venture capital firm and sold to a large company. For the remaining box, technical wizardry, Kraft found a friend of a friend, Will Glaser, who was a brilliant engineer and experienced founder. The result was a much more solid and well-rounded foundation than if Westergren had succumbed to the like-seeks-like tendencies that often breed fragile foundations for teams.[15]

This straightforward use of a checklist—which is quite different from the use of checklists popularized by Atul Gawande[16]—is one of the most effective ways to counter the magnetic pull of homophily, whether in project teams at work or community activities. As did Westergren, start by creating a list of the capabilities that will be the most important to complete the endeavor effectively. If your initial list is long, prioritize the items so that you can narrow your focus to the most important. If it's a long-term project, allocate the check boxes to different horizons: "Need now," "Need six months from now," and so on. Check off the boxes that you can cover yourself. For the unchecked boxes, and especially for those that are "Need now" or close to it, think about where you can find people (or people who know people) who will be able to fill each box and how you might be able to attract them to the effort. The goal is to end up with one check mark in each box, no double-checked boxes (double-checked boxes are a signal of potentially dangerous overlap), and no high-priority boxes left unchecked (in other words, no gaping holes in the team).

A number of years ago when I was helping found a boys' high school (see Chapter 2), I noticed that the parents who shaped the school's mission and strategy were very similar in work backgrounds (professionals, most with business or health care backgrounds) and religious orientation (Orthodox Jews). When it came time to form the board of directors, we might have faced the problems of homophilic teams if we had limited our scope to our original group. Recognizing this, we created a checklist of capabilities that we wanted within the board: expertise in governance, budgeting, construction, debt financing, fundraising, education, and organizing events. Among the initial group of parents, we were able to check off three of the boxes. For the remaining gaps, we had to brainstorm about other people—often two or three network connections away from us—who might be able to fill those holes. Doing so led us to several new and valuable people, enabling us to avoid gaping holes (such as the construction knowledge necessary to find a location and build a building) and forcing us to diversify (for example, by finding people who knew best practices from non-Orthodox schools) where we might have been tempted to have redundancies.

Checklists are best complemented by another practice, one that brings other people and their points of view into the process: establishing regular check-ins. Chapter 5 shows how venture capitalists have much lower investment success when they give in to homophily by engaging in collaborations driven by affinity-based characteristics. The more the venture capitalists shared affinity-based characteristics, the worse their investment performance. The main cause is poor decision making due to the desire to conform socially and to think alike.[17] When making decisions, they don't sufficiently consider the disadvantages of their favored option and disregard advice from outside experts. They also may lower their expected-return hurdles (how high their expected performance gains should be) and due-diligence standards (how closely they scrutinize each potential investment) to coinvest with investors similar to them.

Leading venture capital firms, cognizant of these challenges, design formal processes to reduce their impact on firm performance. The firms try to ensure that individual partners cannot make investments solely on their own. For instance, they hold weekly meetings, often on Monday mornings, in order to discuss potential deals and whether to invest.[18] The meetings provide a deal-assessment opportunity for partners who have not developed relationships with potential coinvestment partners. To further counter the lowering of due-diligence standards, some firms require deal write-ups that detail specific aspects that might get shortchanged, bringing the biggest potential risks to the attention of the deal champion early on.

Such check-ins are applicable for any business decisions where a "decision champion" is leading the charge and others' perspectives are needed to counter possible bias or ensure that the champion considers a wide variety of important factors. Check-ins can also help at home if one person risks losing perspective during a drawn-out, all-consuming effort such as planning an annual vacation or finding a new house. A partner, family member, or friend can help sort out what has been accomplished so far and how the process is going and perhaps suggest alternative options.

Checklists focus us on what needs to be done. Check-ins keep us honest by involving others whose perspectives aren't skewed by similarity to the people with whom we might collaborate. Together these processes help us avoid the comfortable feeling that comes with associating with compatible others. The most successful entrepreneurs know that friction should be welcomed, as it often leads to even greater productivity. In other words, we need to go for grumpy.

Go for Grumpy

Grumpy isn't easy. Those lunches at USC that I mentioned, for example—the point of the program is to stimulate a free flow of ideas. But in such settings, many of us have trouble getting past our ingrained courtesy. We don't often arrive at the point of tension that stimulates real give-and-take—real learning. Like so many other people, we could learn from entrepreneurs' ability to be blunt when necessary. When John Sculley was resisting Steve Jobs's overtures to leave Pepsi to lead Apple, Jobs famously posed a frank question to him: "Do you want to spend the rest of your life selling sugared water, or do you want a chance to change the world?"[19] The result: Jobs's frank statement jolted Sculley out of his mind-set and inertia and got Jobs the CEO he wanted, at least for the moment.

The most effective entrepreneurs know that their primary goal in seeking collaborators is results, not congeniality. Research by Richard Hackman and his colleagues on professional symphony orchestras actually found a slightly *negative* association between the quality of members' interpersonal relationships and an independent assessment of how the ensembles played together.[20] Grumpy orchestras played together a little better. While conflict can cause unpleasantness, it also fosters learning and increases the likelihood that the team will come up with something creative.

Recognizing this, the best entrepreneurs strive for a diversity of opinions rather than initial harmony, often breeding frustration in the short term but generating better outcomes in the longer term. With each hire they ask themselves: Is my negative reaction to this person due to a difference in style or a disconnect in substance? Remember Tony Tjan's initial, visceral reaction to his section mate's style and how he had to be pushed to overcome it in order to bring aboard a critical member of his team. Conversely, if I'm having a positive reaction to this person, do we really have a distinct, value-adding role to fill, or am I justifying a redundant or irrelevant hire because I feel a kinship?

One reason we are drawn to similar others is the worry that the tensions between us and those who are different from us will be destructive. But by avoiding those disconnects in the short term, we heighten the chances of problems in the longer run. Instead, we need to build our difficult-conversation muscles so we can turn those conversations into productive dialogues.[21]

Seek Good Fights and "Go Ugly Early"

My alum Jessica Alter, CEO of entrepreneurial-networking platform FounderDating, asks would-be cofounders whether their fights tend to escalate rapidly and become knock-down, drag-out affairs. She found that the longer cofounders walk around angry, the more resentments brew and key decisions are postponed.[22] For a rapidly growing startup, such infighting can destroy the interpersonal dynamic so thoroughly that the business ultimately shutters.

If that sounds more like marital advice than business advice, it's because conflict is one of those areas where entrepreneurship has a great deal in common with relationships. Just as in marriage, trivial issues in startups can provoke chronic resentment, ultimately eroding trust. In one startup, the two cofounders fought over whose office would house their joint secretary. In another, disagreements over the company logo sparked friction between the cofounders. That's why the most effective founders learn to raise tough issues without delay. They seem to follow the relationship guidance that one of my students memorably quoted: He said that the best dating advice he had received was to "go ugly early. If your partner can see you at your worst—and still love you—you know you've got a keeper."

Effective founders also learn how to have "good" fights. They avoid what John Gottman, one of the pioneers of modern marital counseling, calls the "four horsemen" of relationship failure: criticism, defensiveness, contempt, and stonewalling. Understanding these markers, which consistently predict divorce with over 90 percent accuracy,[23] helps founders build their difficult-conversation muscles so they can harness differences instead of fearing and avoiding them.

Criticism is the first tactic that couples use in conflict. Instead of attacking the behavior ("Can't you pick up the dishes?"), one person attacks the other's character ("You are so lazy!"). Next in line, defensiveness, is something that most of us have experienced either personally or professionally. We hear something bad about ourselves in a performance review or from our spouse, and we react by blocking out what the other party is saying. "You're late!" sparks "It's not *my* fault that we're always late!" The next horseman, contempt, is the single greatest predictor of divorce. Examples of contempt include responding to a partner's comments with eye rolling, sneering, or even using humor to put your partner down, in addition to more obvious statements such as "You're an idiot." Finally, stonewalling, or nonresponsiveness, occurs when one partner stops cueing to the other that they are following their conversation with verbal affirmations, head nods, or other ways of letting the partner know that they are listening. The presence of these four horsemen predicts early divorcing—within, on average, 5.6 years after the wedding.[24]

A critical part of mastering conflict is pushing yourself to see the other party's point of view. That may sound trite, but this is no small matter—most of us have great difficulty seeing things from others' perspectives. When I randomly assign students to roles as different types of founders in an exercise on negotiating equity splits, I find that the "business" founders cannot grasp the viewpoints of the "techie" founders, and vice versa. The business founders often put down the techies with a tart "You programmers are a dime a dozen!" and the techies fire back with "You've got the easy job in this team!" And that's just within a randomly assigned simulation.

The Ockham founding team's ownership arrangement was a model of antifragility in Chapter 4. Arriving at the agreement required a very difficult conversation between the cofounders. One of the cofounders who had decided to work for the startup full time, Jim Triandiflou, had worked closely with Ken Burows, whose idea had sparked the venture. Triandiflou admits that Burows was "the real entrepreneur" on the team. Burows was slated to be the company's chief operating officer, but Triandiflou had doubts that Burows would be committed to Ockham. First, Triandiflou knew that Burows was enjoying his job (and the assured paycheck) at professional-services firm KPMG. Second, Burows had become a first-time father as they were writing their business plan. "He'd do bottles and change diapers while we were talking through the plan," Triandiflou said. Triandiflou put himself in Burows's shoes, looked at his situation, and came away doubting that Burows would want to take on the load of founding a company at the same time as he was founding his family.[25]

Before the team made any plans that might be hard to undo, Triandiflou made sure to raise the sensitive issue of Burows's involvement in Ockham. When Burows announced that he might not be joining the startup, Triandiflou says, "That ticked me off a bit, quite honestly." However, he wanted to avoid sparking defensiveness, so he refrained from letting Gottman's horseman of criticism trample the relationship. As a result, they were able to craft the ownership agreement that enabled the team to get stronger from what could have been a devastating defection. Burows invested capital in the company to help it through its initial funding challenges, and in the longer term, Triandiflou says, "We ended up staying friends, and our families still vacation together."[26]

For founders, understanding others' viewpoints is a necessity. Indeed, for Ockham, it could have been a matter of business survival. When the best founders are going to pitch to a potential investor, they look at their slides and presentation through the investor's eyes; when they are trying to hire a chief technology officer who works at a large company, they try to tune in to how that person might want to have a greater impact by working in a startup.

Gottman uses the term "masters of marriage" to describe couples who manage to avoid the horsemen and maintain fairness during conflict. They're able to nurture a culture of appreciation composed of "respect, gratitude, affection, friendship, and noticing what's going right." Gottman describes this as a habit that can be cultivated. These "master" couples do have conflicts, but even if they argue frequently, they treat each other as good friends.[27] "When the masters of marriage are talking about something important, they may be arguing, but they are also laughing and teasing, and there are signs of affection because they have made emotional connections," says Gottman.[28]

Masters-of-marriage couples boast a ratio of five positive interactions for every negative interaction. Couples with a positive to negative interaction ratio lower than 5:1 raise their risk of divorce. Common positive interactions such as a smile or a warm touch neutralize strong negative actions very effectively. Couples who fight a lot can still be "masters of marriage"—if they have at least five times as much positive passion running through their marriage.[29]

Just as there are masters of marriage, there are founders like Jim Triandiflou, who master the subtleties of their relationships with cofounders, investors, and other stakeholders. Like marriage masters, they not only avoid criticism and other negative behaviors; they also create an atmosphere of respect and appreciation. Some of them also successfully navigate a duo of other minefields: involving family members in their businesses and succumbing to the cultural imperative to apportion responsibilities and rewards along strictly egalitarian lines. But as we see in later chapters, these minefields are some of the trickiest that founders—and we—face.

CHAPTER 7

ARE YOU PLAYING WITH FIRE AND OVEREMPHASIZING EQUALITY?

YOU MAY HAVE NOTICED, over the course of this book, a gradual progression in my discussions of life challenges and the founder wisdom that applies to them. In the discussion of the stories of Caroline and Akhil, my advice tends toward the black and white: Don't let psychic handcuffs progressively prevent you from fulfilling your dreams. If you're too passionate, rein in your impulse to leap. I show that it's a mistake to dread failure or to neglect to plan for success.

As the book moves forward into subtler issues such as reliance on mental blueprints, the categorical outlines by necessity begin to blur. Black and white begin to fade. Our mental patterns may limit us, but they provide many benefits as well. The same is true of our affiliations with people similar to us.

Now we arrive at a pair of challenges that are even more subtle. With greater subtlety comes controversy.

First, whenever we embark on a new venture that requires a solid foundation, whether it's a physical move, a new job, a creative project, or something else, we often face a powerful magnetic pull to involve family or close friends in our endeavors. Is giving in to that pull a good idea or a bad idea? "Good idea," some will answer, especially those who have already embarked on an endeavor with such compatriots. "It depends," others will answer. True, but dangerous if we use that as a reason for inaction, either because we think we'll beat the odds or because it's hard to define what it depends on. Unfortunately, as illustrated in this chapter, the answer is usually not what we hope it will be, making inaction problematic. Fortunately, though, there are solutions to many of the challenges we can cause for ourselves when we succumb to this magnetic pull, as long as we face up to the risks we are taking.

Second, many of us live in cultural environments that emphasize strict equality in relationships, roles, and rewards. Is strict equality a good idea or a bad idea? People have strong feelings about this question, too. We will delve into what can make it a problematic approach to decision making and see the actions we should take to resist its magnetic pull.

In this chapter we leave black and white far behind and go deep into gray.

PLAYING WITH FIRE

The people close to us loom large in our lives—parents, siblings, children, aunts and uncles, cousins, childhood companions, college friends, military buddies, or other friends. These individuals may have given us their share of trouble, but they know us deeply, and no doubt more than a few of them have helped us out of past jams. Therefore it only stands to reason that we might be inclined to work with or for some of them, or otherwise enlist a few of them in meeting our goals. The allure of collaborating with those very close to us can sometimes be irresistible.

The story of ProLab, a medical laboratory-services company in Texas, illustrates both the hopes and the reality of collaboration with family members. Hillary Mallow had become CEO of ProLab after its founder, at age forty-five, unexpectedly suffered a fatal heart attack while golfing. As ProLab grew, Mallow told me, "I couldn't handle everything that was on my plate. [But] we didn't have the money to hire high-level people."[1]

Her husband, who had been a high-performing partner at a prominent consulting firm, had decided to leave his job, and Mallow brought him into the business to help out. The timing seemed opportune. "I knew [he] was really smart. He had a lot of knowledge to bring to the table, a lot of experience at [his firm] dealing with different situations—he would drive projects, overhaul companies, helping them improve different aspects. . . . I had faith that we would be a team." His involvement in the business would also help synchronize their home and work lives: "We had two kids, and my husband had been constantly traveling for work. I thought this could be a great partnership—he wouldn't be traveling anymore, and we could work together on who's picking up the kids which days and who's managing what at work." They decided to become "couple-preneurs": significant others who work together in a startup.

Over the initial months, Mallow's husband increased ProLab's financial discipline and eventually took on the chief financial officer role. However, tensions began to rise within the team, exacerbated by ProLab's first annual loss. As work stresses grew, "Work was coming home with us. Happy talk and funny talk at home became stressful talk, all about work. . . . [My husband's] favorite saying became, 'I work for my wife 24/7.'"

Mallow soon realized that she had never really seen the work side of her husband. His personality at work was quite different from what it had been at home. Afraid of the impact their workplace disagreements would have on their home life, Mallow stopped trying to resolve work disagreements with him: "I stopped standing up to him because I didn't want to cause problems in our marriage. I was worried about having a fight at work, knowing it would come home and we would continue the fight at home." She reflected, "You walk into your house and at some point at night you're looking at each other. You still have that conflict that emerged at work. As much as you try to put it aside, you can't help but be looking at the same person you just had that issue with."

Over the next few weeks, the communication tensions rose and company performance fell. "We were not a team anymore. We had stopped doing update meetings like we used to do. I wasn't watching the finances by the time we got to that point; [he] was managing it. I should have pushed to see the finances. But I was trying to be calm and save whatever relationship [we] had left. I didn't want to push it."

Her assessment of what she should have done was spot on because, in 2007, her accountant called, telling Mallow that ProLab was nearing insolvency; the company had lost $1.3 million. "I truly believed that we'd never get to that point," Mallow says, "but it came: 'Is the business going to fail because we won't fire my husband?' Then, the decision was, 'OK, we fire my husband now.'"

The emotional contagion from working together and the firing decision spread beyond the company into their personal lives. Soon after firing him, Mallow filed for divorce. Despite all of the potential value that her husband would have added to the company, the destructive effects of involving him had negated that value. Within a few years, the company was back in the black, but the marriage was over. Indeed, family-business researcher Gibb Dyer and his colleagues found that across seventy-one companies in which owner-managers had brought in their spouses to help, there was no improvement in business performance, and the owner-managers were unlikely to even accept advice from their spouses. Often, the spouse would leave the company after only a year or two.[2] (Ironically, one of Dyer's coauthors on the study was his own son.)

Integrating the people we know best into our business lives seems like a no-brainer, especially if we don't have the time or money to run extensive network searches. In the business world, family firms are beloved. We should not allow that to blind us to the fact that we often hear about only the prominent ones that succeed. The more common failures are often (understandably) covered up by the players involved.

My data show that professional collaboration with family members and close friends is one of the riskiest moves an entrepreneur can make. This jumps out when I graph the stability of founding teams that include social ties (friends or family) and those that don't. After an initial honeymoon period during which the lines are statistically indistinguishable from each other, they diverge markedly, with significantly worse stability within the social teams. Each additional personal relationship within a team increased the likelihood that a cofounder would leave—rarely a good sign for a team, and especially for one composed of friends in which we would expect team cohesion to be prized—by 28.6 percent.[3]

Most striking given our assumptions about the benefits of engaging with those we "know," social teams are even less stable than teams composed of strangers or acquaintances. Apparently, when we collaborate with those closest to us socially, we're actually starting in negative territory—we have to undo many of the negative effects of our prior relationships—compared to strangers and acquaintances, with whom we are starting at ground zero.

Involving friends and family is more endearing but often less enduring.

Many of us have seen or heard examples of these perils. When I ask audiences of future founders to vote on whether startup teams composed of friends or family would be more or less stable than other founding teams, the hands that indicate "less stable" always vastly outnumber the others. So we should find few social teams among high-potential startups, right? Especially given that these teams must deal with the complexities of fast-moving markets and that they have access to professional guidance on team building? But no. My data show that 43 percent of teams in high-tech and life-sciences startups had cofounders who knew each other socially but not professionally before founding, and 12 percent had cofounders who were relatives.[4] In other words, despite knowing better, more than half of these founding teams were unable to resist the magnetic pull of tapping friends and family. (And there's an even higher percentage of such teams in small businesses and, not surprisingly, family businesses![5])

When we involve friends and family, we are playing with fire. Much as the fire of a blacksmith hardens and strengthens a metal tool, we hope that collaborating with friends and family will forge a strong team. Yet when you play with fire, you can also get burned, as did Hillary Mallow. We may become close to our coworkers once we have established a solid professional foundation for our relationship, but that's very different from involving friends and family in our professional endeavors. As John D. Rockefeller said, "A friendship built on business can be glorious, while a business built on friendship can be murder."[6]

Mallow's experience highlights four major risks of involving family or close friends in our endeavors: Relatives can surprise us by acting differently than we expect; we tend not to vet those we love; we often avoid difficult conversations with people close to us; and damage in one realm, whether it's the family setting or the endeavor, has a tendency to spread. Let's look at each of these in turn.

The surprise factor People assume, on the basis of experience at home, that they know how a family member or friend will act, for example, in a work setting. But people often act very differently in other compartments of life. For example, in a study by Stanford researchers Peter Belmi and Jeffrey Pfeffer, people primed to think of themselves in an organizational context (as a coworker) reciprocated less than those in an otherwise parallel personal situation (as a friend or acquaintance). In other words, individuals show markedly less willingness to offer favors in their work lives than in their personal lives.[7] We can't necessarily count on the support we get in one setting to map onto the next; yet we often fail to realize that.

Failure to vet When considering a potential collaboration with someone you don't know, you probably tread carefully with eyes wide open, watching for signs of incompatibility, assessing whether the person's capabilities are up to the task, and being willing to abandon the interaction if it doesn't seem to be working. However, when we think we know a person well, we act very differently, assuming that the capabilities and compatibility are there and never even considering abandoning the effort. We dive in blindly without doing basic vetting. Realistically, though, compared to all of the people you might be able to tap across your network, what are the chances that that your friend or family member is really the best person for a particular role?

Talking about tough issues Many of us have a hard time facing difficult conversations—emotionally charged interactions laden with uncertainty[8]—with the people who are close to us. We romantically think that spouses working together is a utopian situation that helps create a perfect blend of family and work, with common goals, dreams, and ideals. Some people do, indeed, find it easier to have difficult conversations with those close to them. However, for most of us, those conversations come with a great deal of pressure that leads us to avoid having them. We avoid expressing negative information, fear the negative consequences of raising sensitive issues, and don't want to disappoint family members.[9] We resist those conversations until the point where either we can no longer push them off or we harm our relationship. The more difficult the issue, the more we use negative words when discussing it, injecting criticism, contempt, and defensiveness into our interactions and decreasing satisfaction with the state of the relationship.[10]

This pattern of avoiding difficult conversations emerges early in a relationship. Credit-reporting firm Experian conducted a survey of 1,002 American couples who had gotten married in 2015. The consistent pattern was that the couples had a difficult time discussing financial issues. Even though a majority of respondents agreed with the statement "Before I was married, I considered how a potential spouse's credit score could affect my finances," that consideration was not backed up by actual conversations about financial issues. Thirty-three percent of the newlyweds were surprised by their partners' financial situations, and 36 percent didn't know anything about the partners' spending habits. Forty percent did not know their partners' credit scores before becoming married, and one quarter did not know their spouses' annual incomes. A full 39 percent of the newlyweds had already suffered additional marital stress because of their credit scores.[11]

Spillover If tensions are heightened within one realm of the relationship, those tensions are likely to damage another unless they are addressed, as we saw with Hillary Mallow. Psychologists Linda Dezső and George Loewenstein studied nearly one thousand cases of people making personal loans to friends—mixing a business transaction with their personal lives. They found that the arrangements were likely to be informal, that borrowers would recall having paid back a larger proportion of the loan than they had, and that "borrowers have a blind spot when it comes to recognizing the negative feelings and perceptions evoked in lenders by delinquent loan repayment."[12] The result was that the loans, particularly those not paid off in time, would have destructive effects on the personal relationship between the formerly close friends.

The consequences can be far reaching. Studies on social ties by network researcher David Krackhardt of Carnegie Mellon suggest that unanticipated changes to your relationship in one realm (e.g., newly disagreeing with each other at work) could provoke backlash in another realm (spillover fighting at home).[13] Our fear of causing damage to one or the other relationship is yet another factor leading us to push off having difficult discussions until the point where real damage occurs. The fact that we now have two big arenas of potential tensions, such as the social and the professional, also increases the chances of having problems and exacerbates their repercussions.

I regularly feel this tension between the personal and professional. One summer, one of my daughters worked as an intern for me. Whenever she was around, I found myself being much more self-conscious about my interactions with my colleagues and my employees. I was concerned that how she saw me at the office might affect how she viewed me at home and that my communications with my employees might be less clear because her presence skewed how I dealt with them. In addition, what would happen if (when?) she missed the target on a challenging new project and needed some constructive criticism to improve? Would I be able to provide it? I didn't think I could. I also was pretty sure that she wouldn't be able to hear my guidance as constructive criticism. Maybe, I thought, I should begin a new movement: Don't You Dare Take Your Daughter to Work Day!

Entrepreneurs know the risks of involving friends or family in their endeavors. Rather, I should say they "know" the risks; they're quick to acknowledge them. Remember the resounding show of hands when I ask entrepreneurship audiences about how stable friends-and-family teams will be. Moreover, entrepreneurs are conversant with high-profile toxic examples, such as the tale of the Guccis. The story has a Shakespearean sweep, but the outlines of it are that Gucci, built by Italian dishwasher-turned-entrepreneur Guccio Gucci in 1921, became a fashion powerhouse in the late 1950s and 1960s when Jacqueline Kennedy and Elizabeth Taylor were photographed wearing its products. In 1953, after Guccio's death, ownership passed equally to his three sons, one of whom later died, leaving the company split between Aldo and Rodolfo. Other voices demanding a say in decision making were silenced. After trying to create his own line within Gucci and to modernize the business, Aldo's son Paolo was fired.[14] He responded by divulging financial information that sent Aldo to prison for tax evasion.

With Aldo out and Rodolfo now dead, the next generation began to struggle for power, and profits suffered. Family members reached out to private equity for a rescue. One investor reported with amazement, after meeting with a Gucci scion: "He's being sued by his relatives, his shares have been sequestered, and he doesn't even have control! The tremendous infighting between him and his relatives is all over the papers."[15] It was only after investors purchased the company (at a steep discount) and reorganized it with no family members in positions of authority that the brand returned to powerhouse status.

Yet I put quotation marks around "know" above when I say entrepreneurs know this, because my research shows that many entrepreneurs continually involve themselves with people close to them anyway. This makes it even more critical for us to find firewalls they can put in place when they are playing with fire.

Pause for Reflection

- When you were younger and you saw one of your parents—your mother, say—in a professional context, such as on Take Your Child to Work Day, did you notice that she acted differently than at home?

    - Did she deal with workplace subordinates the same way she dealt with you and your siblings at home or toward her spouse or her own siblings? If not, why do you think those differences emerged?

- Are there ways in which *you* act differently between the work and personal contexts? Are you less or more assertive at work? Less or more willing to forgive mistakes?

I am not downplaying the advantages that can be derived from working with close friends and relatives. My family is my own top priority. (This kind of prioritization makes it even more important to ensure that we don't get burned when we engage with them.) Indeed, one of the purposes of this book is to help you strengthen the ties within your immediate family by reducing the stress around difficult decisions, changes, and dynamics. Of course, there are many examples of family teams that have done great things. When we involve close friends or relations in our endeavors, we all hope that we will become one of those exceptional examples. Unfortunately, we're more likely to see firsthand why those cases are exceptions.

Hillary Mallow became one of the cautionary tales of involving family in her venture. Yet, despite the debacle with her husband, she found room in Pro-Lab for her mother, who was feeling burned out after working for thirty years as a dental hygienist and was looking to change gears. As discussed in Chapter 8, with her mother Mallow used a very different arrangement than the one she used with her husband—and this new arrangement worked far better than the failed one.

As does Mallow, we all love to share our peak experiences with the people we care about. Indeed, the motivation to share with them plays a part in the egalitarian bias that so often hampers founders and nonfounders alike.

OVEREMPHASIZING EQUALITY

Everyone seeks fair treatment. That's a given. But there's a problem with fairness: Our perceptions of it are highly subjective. We all have different definitions of it, and those definitions change over time. So we search for objective markers of fairness that are easily measured. Often the marker we seize on is equality. We look for differences between people's rewards or responsibilities; if there are none, all is equal, which we deem to be fair.

For example, if I have a colleague whose qualifications match mine, I want our salaries and benefits to be the same. In gauging my employer's fairness, I focus not so much on the dollar amount of my compensation as on the gap between my colleague and myself. If it's zero, I'm satisfied.

Over and over again, equal becomes a stand-in for fair. The substitution is reinforced from childhood. Try to remember what it was like as a four-year-old at a birthday party. You see one glorious cupcake remaining on the serving plate but two of you without a treat. Perhaps you try to yank it away; maybe your friend gets to it first. One of you cries foul, most likely in tears. Adults quickly intervene, and an age-old lesson is passed on again: *Equal sharing is best.* Someone divides the cupcake, each of you gets half, and the problem is solved. (When you get more sophisticated and don't have an adult nearby to intervene, one of you cuts the cupcake in half, and the other picks which piece to get. Equal!) The cupcake will be quickly forgotten, but the lesson about sharing will be reinforced throughout your early life until it becomes one of the strongest elements of your blueprint, an assumption or outlook that goes unquestioned.

The blueprint is strengthened as we continue to hear about people and institutions insisting on equality as a proxy for fairness. Schools, for example, impose core-curriculum and minimum-proficiency standards to eliminate perceived educational inconsistencies and ensure that all students learn the same things. Obvious disconnects in this logic arise all the time: Teachers realize there's no sense in giving diversely talented pupils equally challenging assignments. Coaches don't give athletes equal playing time. Choruses can't feature all singers as soloists. Nevertheless, equality remains so powerfully associated with fairness that we continue to see it as the ideal state and attempt to apply it to many areas of our lives. Within the committees that we form with peers at work or in our extracurricular activities, the pull of equality can be very strong. We are inclined to say, "We're all in this together, and each decision will be better if we engage as equals." It's the principle of one person, one vote. That's fairness.

Founders often experience this magnetic pull. With "All for one and one for all" as their implicit mantra, many entrepreneurs try to architect equal teams. Cofounders on their teams receive "C-level" titles in which everyone is a "chief something officer." Even when there is a chief executive officer who is supposed to have more weight than the other "chiefs," teams adopt collective decision-making rules dominated by equality in the form of "one founder, one vote," decision making by consensus, or majority rule. All cofounders are involved in every major decision. Such teams are likely to reinforce this role equality by adopting reward equality in which everyone holds the same amount of equity ownership (recall the Three Rs, discussed in Chapter 6).

This is particularly problematic within the most common size of founding team, two people, which happens in nearly 40 percent of the startups in my data set.[16] If the two cofounders disagree, how can a team emphasizing equality resolve the gridlock of a 1–1 decision? For that matter, how can married couples emphasizing equality resolve their own 1–1 gridlocks without heightened tensions?

The magnetic pull of equality can cause problems even for those leading the largest of companies. Researchers Ryan Krause, Richard Priem, and Leonard Love examined the executive teams of publicly traded US companies and found seventy-one companies in which two people had shared the title of co-CEO for a sustained period.[17] Such arrangements existed atop companies rang-ing from Whole Foods and IMAX to Bed Bath and Beyond. The researchers noticed that some of the co-CEO relationships were indeed partnerships of equals but that others were relatively unequal despite the co-CEO titles. They decided to see how well those different arrangements performed.

When the co-CEOs had equal influence, company performance (in this case, measured using return on equity—ROE) was slightly negative. Companies that divided power equally between the co-CEOs were "bogged down in power struggles." As the gap in influence widened, company performance increased significantly, to an ROE of 243 percent. As the gap got very unequal, though, performance turned down, to 209 percent. At this end of the extreme, the dramatic difference in clout eventually resulted in distrust and communication breakdowns. Yet even that weaker performance was significantly above the negative performance of the equal co-CEOs. In their study, the researchers quote the French pioneer of management thinking, Henri Fayol: "A body with two heads is in the social as in the animal sphere a monster, and has difficulty in surviving."[18] Better to have a clear, single head than to have two conflicting heads sharing power.

The pull of equality may be even stronger within our personal lives. If you're married and living in the United States, you're much more likely than in decades past to share the burden of breadwinning with your spouse. US census data tracks the number of households in a "traditional" arrangement—where the husband works full time and the wife stays at home—as well as data on "egalitarian" marriages where both spouses work full time. Between 1976 and 2013, the proportions flipped: Traditional marriages fell from 26 percent of total households to 17 percent, while egalitarian marriages increased from 17 percent to 29 percent.[19]

In *It's Not You, It's the Dishes*, journalist Paula Szuchman describes one such egalitarian couple, Eric and Nancy. "They would say, 'I did the laundry last time—it's your turn.'" They had long chore logs in the kitchen to ensure that no one did more work than the other. When one made dinner, the other would follow suit. Friends marveled at how they defied stereotypes: *Eric knows how to use a Swiffer! Nancy gives him so much space!*[20] To all appearances, they were the perfect egalitarian married couple.

But there was a catch to Eric and Nancy's story: They weren't happy. The long chore list was constantly being updated and reassigned. One night, when Eric was chopping onions for a slow-cooked Moroccan lamb stew, he saw Nancy watching TV and thought to himself, "Why am I spending all of this time on a fancy meal when all she ever makes is mac and cheese?" Nancy liked dog walking, while Eric absolutely hated picking up after the dog. But Nancy refused to do the task every day out of fear that her "hours worked" would exceed Eric's. Tensions like these filled their interactions, making their chore arrangement increasingly unsustainable.[21]

Sociologist Stacy Rogers of Penn State found, similar to the finding with co-CEOs, the *lowest* levels of marital stability in dual-income marriages where the partners made roughly equal amounts. In fact, the odds of divorce were lowest when one spouse made 70 percent or more of the household income. The risk of divorce was highest when wives' and husbands' economic contributions were approximately equal. (Rogers suggests that this is the point at which mutual obligations are weakest.) She posits that egalitarian spouses may end up carefully monitoring who does what at home—much like Eric and Nancy in the example above—leading to periodic renegotiations to maintain their equality, and this endless monitoring heightens tension. Couples whose financial contributions varied had less of a need to keep score in other aspects of their lives.[22]

As my student David discovered (remember from the introduction how David sparked the writing of this book?), a desire for equality can also hinder decision making in a marriage. David was struggling with the pull of equality in the relationship with his new spouse. Both of them had always pictured their ideal marriage as being a partnership of equals. They would take turns doing chores and collaborate on key decisions. On the positive side, when his wife seemed to be doing more than he was, David felt the need to up his game. However, this was accompanied by negative feelings when his spouse seemed to be doing less than he was or when each one had to do a chore at which he or she was weak or didn't enjoy. Their approach meant that they had to discuss a lot more decisions than expected and to face heightened tensions whenever they couldn't agree.

Sometimes the pursuit of equality can set off a series of decisions aimed at ensuring temporary fulfillment for one partner, then the other, then the first again, and so on in a pendulum-like rhythm—with the couple never truly achieving a sense of balance and peace. For instance, my student Angela decided to take a job in New York after college graduation. This posed difficulties for her European-born boyfriend who had already landed his dream offer in Europe. To stay with her, he looked for work in New York but had trouble finding a company willing to sponsor his visa. It took him nearly a year to find a position. It was a less-thrilling position than the one he was giving up, but at least it was a job in his field and in the same city as his girlfriend.

Now that her boyfriend had made sacrifices for her, Angela felt pressure to reciprocate. She thought that he would "expect some sort of accommodation on my end for the next milestone of our lives," which might mean relocating to Europe or the United Kingdom, where conditions for both finding a job and working would probably be less than ideal for her career.

Even if we believe that in the long run everyone's effort levels and contributions will even out, we still have trouble dealing with short-term mismatches in efforts and rewards. A student who had been married for several years said to me, "Both my wife and I have had times when we raised the issue that we felt bad because chores were starting to feel less equal. Even when one of us argues that it's because of a unique situation—for example, 'I've just been extra busy lately'—it rarely solves the problem. It's hard to fight the natural instinct of getting upset when something feels uneven."

This is also true within startup teams, where the importance of each founder's tasks can ebb and flow. For instance, the online investor network Up-Down was founded by three people: Michael and Georg, who were the business cofounders, and Phuc, the technical cofounder. The team had agreed on an equal split of the ownership, except for a small reward for idea guy Michael. While Michael was spending weeks documenting customers' needs, Phuc had little to do. Even though Phuc's cofounders understood the situation and recognized that he would inevitably do more later, they grumbled at seeing his contributions ebb. (Because of family commitments, Georg had not been able to work on the venture much, either.) Michael began having severe doubts about his cofounders. He told me: "I am kind of scared whether this is the right team to work with if already now their commitment, or the amount of work, is not at the same level as mine!" These tensions prompted Michael to send his cofounders a pointed proposal to fundamentally reallocate their ownership stakes. He reduced Phuc's percentage significantly (and Georg's by a smaller amount), prompting a crisis as Phuc felt disrespected and seriously considered leaving the startup, while Michael vowed not to continue if the ownership stakes were not adjusted.

The expectation of sustained equality can persist and damage partnerships even when couples are not initially aware of its role in their relationship. Stanford sociologist Brooke Conroy Bass found that many married couples try to share household responsibilities equally—until the birth of their first child.[23]

At that point, the equal division of labor often breaks down as women assert control over childrearing. So-called alpha moms want their babies cared for in a specific way. Fathers, having lost their say, withdraw, often reluctantly. Resentment builds among women even though they pushed for greater control, as both parents report violated expectations. At four months postpartum, these mothers reported having less relationship satisfaction and more depression.[24]

The ambiguities in the topic of equality are deep and wide. Admittedly, equal sharing of rewards and responsibilities can be beneficial, by heightening engagement that motivates and attracts better participants to an endeavor. Moreover, it simply feels good to know that we're square. Once we split the tab or the dog-walking chores or the proceeds of selling the temperamental snow blower we bought in partnership with our neighbor, we feel unburdened—there's nothing hanging over us. However, as we have seen, the pursuit of equality can have the opposite effect from the one we intended, heightening our need to understand how we can apply founding best practices to this realm of our lives, too.

Pause for Reflection

- Have you tried to establish equality of roles, rewards, or responsibilities in an endeavor? For instance, did you and a partner apportion equal tasks to yourselves in launching a charitable project, renovating a home, or starting a band?

  - Did your emphasis on equality lead you to monitor who did what and when? Was that monitoring beneficial, or did unnecessary tensions arise as a result?

- Did you stop to ask yourself whether it was equality that you were really looking for, or was it actually fairness?

  - If the latter, were there ways to achieve fairness other than strict egalitarianism?

CHAPTER 8

FIGHT THE MAGNETIC PULLS OF FAMILY AND EQUALITY

ENTREPRENEURS HAVE a complicated relationship with the public. On the one hand, the public is critical to their success, and entrepreneurs know it. Without potential buyers there would be no new startups. Public opinion is constantly on their minds. Would-be founders typically spend years trying to anticipate the desires of the masses—what services the Consumer Nation might be willing to pay for and what products a given market might want, even if it doesn't yet know it wants them.

On the other hand, many entrepreneurs have an instinctive aversion to herd psychology. They may cultivate an exceptional understanding of what the public is thinking, but that doesn't mean that they share its sentiments, outlook, or conventional wisdom. Just the opposite, in fact. As we see throughout this book, and as we see to an even greater degree in this chapter, successful entrepreneurs are quick to identify and reject the prevailing views of the crowd. If anything, contrary-minded entrepreneurs see their crowd-countering tendencies as a potential advantage in the entrepreneurial world. They maintain a healthy distance from friends and family members, and they depart from strict egalitarianism in divvying tasks, risks, and rewards.

AVOID THE TIES THAT BLIND

The most challenging friends-and-family situations are those in which professional and personal connections overlap, and the two relationships are inconsistent—or conflict. When Hillary Mallow brought on her husband as a

ProLab employee reporting directly to her, their new professional relationship was inconsistent with their existing peer-to-peer relationship of husband and wife. She had hoped that involving him in the company would help both at work and at home. However, she was blind, both willingly and involuntarily, to the risks she was taking. She didn't anticipate that he'd behave differently in the office than at home. She avoided conversations about work problems for fear that she would harm their marriage, and she didn't take steps to reduce the personal repercussions if things went sour at work. The result was a devastating divorce that also imperiled ProLab.

Despite the debacle with her husband, Mallow still found room in ProLab for her mother, a longtime dental hygienist looking to make a career change.[1] Bringing her mom into the business was potentially even more dangerous. For one thing, their hierarchical (even biological) mother-daughter relationship completely conflicted with their new employee-employer relationship.

Hillary Mallow didn't start ProLab; she was an early employee unexpect-edly thrust into a leadership role. But having become CEO, she had to take on a founder mind-set—ProLab was still young and faced many of the early-stage uncertainties of startups. Fortunately, Mallow took a very different approach with her mom than she had with her husband. By doing so, she re-duced the chances that she would get burned when she played with fire. Mal-low's approach highlights several best practices that will help us avoid getting burned, too.

Date Family and Friends (Maybe Even More than Strangers)

Mallow at first hired Mom on a part-time basis. Given her experience with patient charts and dental-office management, Mom's first role was as a facili-ties auditor, in which she visited clients and reviewed their patient records to ensure they matched ProLab's records. Over time Mallow was able to test and confirm her expectation that Mom "was responsible, had a lot of experience, was very personable, caring, and giving. I could trust her to do what needs to be done."[2]

She was also able to assess whether their relationship would be able to handle professional challenges. Mallow insisted on always paying Mom "a fair wage—never more than what we would pay anybody else in the role." Mom said, "I was upset because she knew I wanted the money and I thought, 'Don't you think I deserve a raise?' But I didn't hold a grudge and didn't keep it fester-ing inside of me. She had to be fair to everybody and can't pick me out and give me more money." After more than a year of "dating Mom" and seeing how well she could handle disappointment and sensitive issues, Mallow hired her as a full-time employee.[3]

Mallow had learned two important lessons. First, she realized how strong the temptation is to be lax in scrutinizing a family member. After all, we "know" our relatives already. It's difficult to be skeptical about them or to question them and risk their being hurt by rejection. Consequently, when we work with those close to us, our tendency is to rubber-stamp a collaboration rather than carefully evaluate it.

Second, Mallow realized that ignoring early challenges can set you up for bigger problems down the road. So not only was she just as careful with her mom as she would have been with a stranger, but she also made sure to face the challenge at the beginning of her mother's employment.

Mallow was not alone in creating a step-by-step vetting process for her mother. Before adding even their closest confidants to a team, many effective entrepreneurs make sure to "date" them, trying to assess compatibility as well as complementarity of talents. While struggling to get a cab in San Francisco and again amid a blizzard in Paris, Garrett Camp had an idea for a smartphone-based service that would bring together drivers with paying riders. He began discussing his idea with a wide range of people, four of whom became his personal board of advisors. Those four included an investor in Camp's prior startup, StumbleUpon; a serial entrepreneur; Tim Ferriss, who had recently released a blockbuster book, *The 4-Hour Workweek*; and a new friend named Travis Kalanick. Camp found that "Travis was the best brainstorming partner" and began deepening their relationship.[4] Kalanick became an active advisor with a 10 percent stake in the company, then an unofficial part-time employee, then a full-time member of the team, and then eventually the driver behind what became the world's most valuable startup, Uber (until several years later, when his managerial driving style became perilous and he was forced out). Such dating enables entrepreneurs to see where they might be blindsided by their assumptions about how friends and relatives would function as part of their team.

Moreover, to prepare for any inauspicious revelations that might come up during the dating process, successful founders tend to structure their job offers to allow maximum reversibility. Rather than having the new hire dive in fully, a founder may set up a project with a strict time limit, clear assessments, and a concrete exit plan. For example, a founder might schedule a two-month evaluation, with no expectation of the friend or relative's continued participation. You can adopt a similar approach in many potential collaborations. Is there a well-defined subset of tasks that will help you move the project forward? Can it be given a defined end date? If so, then clearly set the expectation that you will work on this subproject together, and at the end of it, you'll both assess the pros and cons of the collaboration, give each other feedback on what could be improved, and each decide whether to have a second date. At the end of the subproject, you'll both be far more informed about each other's true strengths and weaknesses than if you had solely relied on your ill-informed hopes. Then if you need to terminate the collaboration, it's a lot less painful early on and may end up saving the personal relationship from irreparable harm down the road.

Your parents' thirtieth anniversary is approaching, and you and your siblings want to make a big surprise party for them. Your youngest sister is keen to take charge, but the rest of you lack confidence in her ability to pull together the caterer, hall, flowers, "This Is Your Life" slideshow, band, invitation list, and invitations. You collectively create a step-by-step process so that you can see how things progress under her lead and, if warranted, change course while the planning is still in the early stages. The plan calls for her to get three bids from caterers and halls while the rest of you get started on other tasks, and you schedule a check-in for two weeks later.

At that check-in meeting, to assess how things are going, list the three biggest surprises or challenges that came up during this initial phase. After discussing them during your check-in meeting, delve into how you might be able to address the challenges and assess whether the benefits of working together outweigh the potential problems. For instance, if your sister got the three bids but neglected a key detail—where is Mom's beloved walnut rugelach in the dessert order?—the check-in might include a (tactful) conversation about the value of checklists. Your sister, meanwhile, might (equally tactfully) point out that in fulfilling your task of tracking down your parents' college friends, you and your brother neglected to get e-mail addresses. Having learned more about each of your strengths and weaknesses, and having seen whether each sibling is able to take criticism constructively, you can collectively decide whether your sister should take on greater responsibility, if that's what she still wants. She can choose another set of tasks to be accomplished during another short time frame—maybe listening to band candidates—while you and your brother start collecting pictures for the slideshow. And getting those e-mail addresses!

Her listening to band candidates could be a great plan unless, of course, your sister is tone deaf. A misfit between role and strengths increases the chances that a person will underperform and harm the initiative (or, worse, anniversary party)—and, potentially, your relationship.

If It's Not a Good Fit, Resist

"Nothing destroys trust faster than incompetence," observes organizational psychologist David Javitch.[5] The risk of incompetent performance by a relative is heightened by a bad role assignment that can either lead to your minimizing any errors your relative makes (harming the endeavor) or result in your becoming excessively critical of the relative's performance (harming the cherished relationship). Either situation is asking for trouble, and might result in both forms of harm.

For instance, even though Mallow's husband's strengths lay in information technology, she let him take on the role of ProLab's chief financial officer. As a result, the company dug itself $2 million into debt, its credit line disappeared, and it neared insolvency. As ProLab began to experience financial difficulties that Mallow's husband wasn't able to solve, those difficulties began souring their relationship within the company and frayed their relationship outside it.

By contrast, Mallow insisted on not assigning her mother to a role that would be a misfit for her strengths or would cause unwise pressures within the company. Mom's initial role tapped her decades of experience with patient records. After that, Mom wanted roles that either did not exist or were unavailable at the time. Mallow fought her natural inclination to give in, telling her mom: "I love you, but you know I can't make a role for you or that I don't have that role available." Another time, she agreed that Mom's requested role would be "nice" for the business and paused to think about it but then declined to create it: "It's just not economical, and I'm not going to make it happen." Each time their interpersonal dynamic was a critical ingredient to moving on, as Mallow observed: "Mom was respectful of my decision, and we didn't have any hard feelings about it."[6]

These dialogues can be quite difficult, even—or especially—for a loving mother and child. However, if the initial fit is poor, your incidents of disagreement are likely to become even bigger and more frequent, making the incidents into battles and the battles into wars. The difficult-conversation muscles you are building will be in for an even tougher workout. Even if you believe the fit is there, though, don't let down your guard; discuss potential disconnects and how you can create firewalls to guard both the professional endeavor and your personal relationship.

Create Firewalls and Disaster Plans

Even when the fit initially looks good, avoid wearing rose-colored glasses. Instead, much as we did with crafting antifragile arrangements, envision potential negative scenarios and the necessary actions if each scenario becomes reality. For instance, who will have the final say in case you disagree? In the extreme, who will leave the project if tension-filled gridlock emerges? If you were fighting at home and you walk into the office together, will you really be able to interact professionally with each other? If you disagree at the office, will you be able to keep it from getting personal? One model for this is Sittercity, a pioneer among online matchmakers bringing together parents needing sitters and those willing to work for them. It was founded by entrepreneur Genevieve Thiers, who brought her then-boyfriend, Dan Ratner, into the business to be its technical lead. This couple-preneur team provides us with important best practices.

The first was their mind-set as they embarked on the collaboration. In contrast to focusing on rosy scenarios, Ratner explained to me that they decided to "be prepared for a rough start. Have a disaster plan in place." Their disaster plan called for Ratner to leave the business if their personal relationship ended or there were problems working together. They were clear that "this is Genevieve's business, and I'm here to help her." (When they got married, their disaster plan manifested in a prenuptial agreement.)

To manage their day-to-day disagreements, they developed a so-called Geneva Convention (or, maybe more appropriate for them, a Genevieve Convention): In the event of a disagreement, they had to write it up and copy the entire executive team. In our conversation, Ratner reflected on its effects: "That forces us to get other people involved and to stay focused on the issues at hand rather than on each other." Similarly, Sam Prochazka, an entrepreneur whose cofounder was his identical twin brother, emphasizes putting everything in writing from the beginning: "Relying on handshake agreements, though tempting, leaves room for interpretation and disaster."[7]

Collaborating on a plan enables buy-in from both sides. Formalizing it helps ensure clarity about its details. Involving others in its implementation helps enforceability while improving clarity.

At ProLab, Mallow was initially her mother's direct supervisor, which introduced the tense conversations between them about roles and salaries. However, as ProLab grew, Mom began reporting to another manager. Mallow realized it felt "way better when she didn't work directly for me." Mom agreed that "it was a lot smoother."[8]

From then on, Mallow made sure to apply such structural firewalls throughout the company, assigning cousins and other family members she hired to nonfamily supervisors. (In my own case, when one of my daughters was creating materials for my course one summer, I had her report to my research assistant rather than to me. She took my RA's guidance far better than she would have taken mine!) On the employee side, Mallow said, "I'm clear and upfront: 'You don't work for me, and it's your manager's job to hire and fire. They decide the pay. They decide everything that you're doing. . . . Don't ask me to step in, don't call me if there's an issue, don't involve me, I don't want to know.'"

On the manager's side, she empowered her managers to treat these new hires the same as anyone else and to utilize the HR policies and rules to discipline and even terminate if they saw fit. If Mallow ever sensed a manager was hesitant to treat one of Mallow's relatives or friends fairly, she'd tell the manager: "You need to do what you need to do. . . . You need to let them go." Mallow also instituted a formal company policy that if someone at ProLab stepped out of line, that person would receive a detailed description of the negative incident, what went wrong, and the individual's role in the event. Mallow avidly sticks to this policy, fearing the consequences of compromising it even once. "I've never saved someone because they were family," she says.

These firewalls were necessary even between ProLab's top managers. Amid a steady increase in the squabbles between her two lab chiefs, who had been best friends before starting to work together, Mallow decided to accelerate opening a new lab in Austin, to which she could assign one of the two chiefs while keeping the other in charge of the Dallas lab. This firewall kept the rivals two hundred miles apart from each other.

At Sittercity, the disaster plan called for Dan to step away from the business if the two partners developed problems working together. At ProLab, Hillary Mallow used a more indirect, yet more objective, way to ensure decision control. She had seen how ProLab's founder had originally owned 51 percent of the business, solidifying his control, while she owned 49 percent. When the founder began transitioning out of the business and sold shares to new partners, Mallow bought another 2 percent of the business from him, bringing her stake to 51 percent and giving her majority ownership in case she needed it to resolve any divisive issues that might arise. Soon after, ProLab's founder passed away unexpectedly, and Mallow was alone atop the organization. When disagreements emerged within the team, Mallow's majority ownership broke any gridlock, thanks to her proactive disaster planning.

Mallow found that her Mom was eager to learn and often wanted to discuss work after hours, blurring the line between business and home. "Instead of going to another employee, I would go to talk with Hillary," her mother said. This led Mallow to strictly enforce another firewall: a rule of not talking about work after 5:00 p.m. They agreed not to talk about work while at home unless the matter was urgent. As Mom explained, "We wanted that mother-and-daughter relationship."

Structural solutions and formal rules about separating the personal from the professional may feel overbearing at first, but they effectively reduce the first major risk of playing with fire, the carryover of tensions from one domain to the other. However, that still leaves the second major risk, of avoiding discussions of the elephants in the room in the hopes that the elephants will disappear of their own accord. Sometimes we can reduce that risk ourselves, but often it takes an outside party to make it happen.

Force Difficult Conversations, or Involve a Third Party Who Will Do So

With her husband, Mallow had avoided difficult conversations, fearing that they would harm their personal relationship. In contrast, before Mom joined, "we had a very upfront and very clear conversation that business is business, personal is personal." Mom felt that she would "be able to separate the two," a common platitude that often falls apart when tested. Fortunately, Mallow and her mom tested this proposition early on. When Mom made an early mistake, Mallow told her, "Mom, that doesn't work!"[9]

For Mom, receiving constructive feedback from her daughter was challenging: "The very first time Hillary gave me feedback, I cried and thought, 'My daughter's disappointed in me!' I didn't want to disappoint her. I was very proud of her and wanted her to be proud of me. But we talked about it and said, 'We've got to switch gears; if we're going to work together we can't take things personally.' Yes, we're mother and daughter, but this is a working relationship."[10]

Sometimes it takes a third party to help you get over the natural aversion to conversations about these sensitive issues. These outsiders should be people who have the respect of both collaborators, understand the pitfalls that might occur, and can get both sides to appreciate the need to proactively address them. If you and your sibling are thinking about splitting a time-share vacation home, consult a common friend who has done likewise so you can tap the lessons she's learned while benefiting from her impartial stance toward each of you. If the two of you collaborated to buy a season ticket to your local basketball team or orchestra but are having trouble deciding how to allocate the best events, ask an uncle you both like to help you split them. Organizational psychologist Javitch encapsulates it as follows: "Empower someone you trust, including another relative, to step in and stop actions that appear to be based on irrational feelings, either positive [or] negative."[11] Third parties can play an important role earlier in the process, too, forcing you to look realistically at negative scenarios and to help you think through potential disaster plans. An impartial referee can also come in handy in case ambiguities emerge and you need someone to make a final decision, or if you agree to an important firewall but fear that neither of you will enforce it yourselves.

For instance, one founder-CEO had hired his son to work in his Chinese company. Eventually, the father promoted the son to an important role in the organization, working directly under him. Unfortunately, the two did not always see eye to eye. The father lamented, "He told me that the way I was managing was not good and that we need a new way of running the production. The first thing that crossed my mind was, 'I changed your diapers when you were running around butt-naked, and now you're telling me what to do!?'" They ended up tapping an intermediary—the founder-CEO's wife—to firmly enforce a no-work-at-home policy, which helped prevent work challenges from spilling over into the personal realm.[12]

An important factor leading us to avoid difficult conversations is that we often overestimate the damage they might cause. For instance, communication researcher Dr. David Keating and his colleagues studied communication within families. Prior to having difficult conversations, the majority of respondents feared negative consequences. However, after completing the conversations, 76.5 percent of respondents reported positive outcomes. Those positive outcomes included the strengthening of family relationships; increased trust, understanding, and open communication; and personal happiness and satisfaction.[13] Succeeding at having a difficult conversation can forge a stronger relationship and help us build our "muscle" for dealing with tension-filled dialogues on important issues. Having a clearer picture of the upside of difficult conversations can help us engage in them more productively.

Underestimating Couple-preneurs

When I worked in venture capital, my firm was as broad an investor as could be. It would look at almost any opportunities—except startups helmed by couples, married or otherwise. It had been burned by investing in teams of significant others, so it had one simple rule: "No couple-preneurs!" I've noticed the same directive at a lot of other venture capital firms for similar reasons.

Years after leaving the firm and studying founders extensively, I came to realize that a no-couple-preneurs rule is a big mistake. True, some married pairs dive into founding without planning, but so do teams of nonrelatives. I've been impressed by couple-preneurs who do it right. They acknowledge that they are playing with fire and then design the mechanisms described here to reduce the risks. In fact, well-structured couple-preneur teams may provide one of the best types of investment opportunities out there because they are shunned by so many other investors despite being even more prepared for life's challenges.

Couples who build firewalls deserve to be in the *Life Is a Startup* Hall of Fame alongside those who proactively escape handcuffs while bringing discipline to their passions, harness failures while preparing for the perils of success, and rework their blueprints while managing the comfort that comes from flocking with similar others.

This brings us to the final magnetic pull that is resisted by the best founders: equal sharing.

RESIST THE ALLURE OF EQUALITY

Initially, many entrepreneurs say something like this to their cofounders: "We're all in this together, and each decision will be better if we engage as equals." They seek to balance their duties and each person's contributions to the collective effort.

I refer to this approach as the *Neverland model* because in Peter Pan's home, there was no adult supervising the children. Strict egalitarianism has a distinct appeal—it allows for flexibility and can unleash a team's collective knowledge. But the need to discuss every decision slows founders down when they should be moving quickly to capture opportunities. As a result, tensions increase and gridlock sets in, especially if the founding team is a duo.[14]

An egalitarian approach to rewards can be even more difficult. Three-quarters of founding teams allocate the ownership stakes among themselves within a month of founding.[15] With the startup's prospects still highly uncertain at that point, founders are likely to rush into a 50-50 equal split, often with a "quick handshake" agreement. This early split is one of the most challenging mistakes to undo later, for social, legal, and tax reasons. It tends to haunt founders for years to come. You have probably already seen one example: the particularly bad early split captured in the Academy Award–winning movie *The Social Network*. The movie details Mark Zuckerberg's ill-advised attempts to undo his early founding mistake at Facebook, where he had allocated a substantial ownership stake to a cofounder he later fired. Moreover, my data show that, despite Facebook's strong performance after the quick handshake, such arrangements typically end up underperforming relative to less egalitarian structures, and teams that adopt them get hit with a sizable "handshake penalty." When they raise their first round of financing, quick-handshake teams receive a valuation that is a nearly half a million dollars lower than the valuation received by teams that avoided the magnetic pull of the quick handshake, *ceteris paribus*.[16]

For these reasons, many entrepreneurs over time develop a healthy wariness of strict egalitarianism. This is definitely not to say that they neglect the importance of fairness. They establish de facto guidelines for following alternate paths to fairness that don't necessarily entail strict equality. These guidelines include creating mini-Zeuses, proactively arranging tiebreakers, focusing on the long term instead of the more-convenient present situation, and finding ways to tag team. As we have seen, cofounder partnerships and personal relationships are parallel in many respects. But nowhere in the field of entrepreneurship are the analogies more striking than in the area of equality.

Create Mini-Zeuses

Having a single "Zeus"—an absolute decision maker, as was the case in the Mount Olympus of mythology—is risky for decision making and dicey for maintaining smooth relations. On the other hand, living in Neverland is a recipe for decision gridlock and holds a greater chance of common-denominator decisions. An alternate solution—one that is more successful within startups and often within couples—is to create a structure of mini-Zeuses. Define clear domains and assign each domain to the person whose expertise or passion matches that domain. Give that person control over the decisions within that domain and resist interfering in domains to which you aren't assigned. Such mini-Zeus structures are often found in the most stable of teams.

Allison and John, a couple who couldn't live together without bickering, epitomize a geographic approach to this problem. One of their chronic squabbles involved her irritation over cleaning up after him and his distaste at being told to pick up after himself. They were unwilling to divorce but needed to reduce their constant arguments. So they settled on a creative solution: They bought a divided loft with separate living spaces for each partner. Allison reflected, "This living arrangement has really helped us solve our issues." Allison and John both cook and clean separately but eat together, eliminating the who-does-what conflict that previously pervaded their home. Now, each party is responsible for his or her own chores. For them, the new arrangement feels "a lot like dating again."[17]

The mini-Zeus structure can also be seen in the case of Pandora Radio, where Tim Westergren was the music-guru cofounder, Jon Kraft the experienced startup executive, and Will Glaser the technical whiz. The team created three well-defined domains—music, business, and technology—and handed control of the decisions in each domain to Westergren, Kraft, and Glaser, respectively. Each mini-Zeus got to decide whom to hire within his domain and how to structure his team. Westergren decided how to build the music catalog, Kraft determined financing strategy, and Glaser made the product-architecture decisions.[18]

The Pandora team was able to have this clear division of labor right from the start. However, had Westergren succumbed to the magnetic pull of homophily and founded with another musician instead, they would not have had a clear division of labor because of their overlapping skills. The team would not have been able to create distinct domains of decision making and would thus have had trouble adopting the mini-Zeus structure. Having clear domains and different experts whose skills mapped to each domain enabled this structure to work for Pandora.

This approach could also be applied to the example of my student David, described in the introduction and Chapter 7, as he was ironing out problems with his new spouse. To David I would say: Until now, you've tried to split things down the middle. Instead, work together to define distinct domains, zoom in on each of your strengths, and map those strengths to domains. If you find that you're strong in the same areas, add on a second criterion. For example, for each area of common strength, which domains do you each enjoy doing or at least don't hate doing? Assign as many remaining domains as possible using this second criterion. Of the still remaining domains, which will include areas in which neither of you is strong or that you both dislike? Would it make sense to outsource these or involve someone else whose strengths match that domain? Once you have a list of assigned and outsourced domains, step back and assess how many domains fall to you and your spouse. If there is a clear imbalance, assign the remaining domains with an eye to bringing more balance to your tasks.

For instance, you and your wife have to cover the family finances, cooking, and cleaning. Your wife is strong at finance and enjoys doing it, so she should take that domain. You are an excellent cook, so you should take care of food acquisition and preparation. Neither of you likes to clean, and there's a cost-effective cleaning service in your apartment building, so consider outsourcing that to the service.

In short, embrace your differences instead of trying to smooth over them or ignore them by dividing everything equally. This will likely result in more confident budgeting and investing, better food on the table, and consistent cleanliness in place of arguments over who should mop the kitchen each week.

The biggest issue you'll face now is what to do when issues *cross* your domains. If you disagree about how to move forward, you'll end up in decision gridlock. That's where proactive tiebreakers come in.

Proactively Arrange Tiebreakers

Commonly, two cofounders make up a founding team, as is the case for nearly 40 percent of startups in my data set. Another 12 percent of teams have four cofounders, so about half of all founding teams are even numbered.[19] In these teams, and in couples, tied votes heighten tensions and slow down decision making. How can these teams get past such impasses?

Within founding teams, gridlock is reinforced and compounded if the team has also adopted ownership equality. One gridlock-breaking approach is to allocate equity unequally or to give only one founder a seat on the board of directors. When couples diverge, they can achieve a similar level of unequal equity by involving a third leg on the stool—an unbiased but informed mentor both partners respect or even their biased and partially informed children—to break the tie. One couple decided that when they disagreed on which restaurant to attend, they would take a page out of the basketball rulebook of alternating sides whenever there is a jump ball. The founding duo in Chapter 7 who disagreed about whose office should house their shared secretary decided to resolve their impasse by flipping a quarter.

Whichever method you choose, the key is to decide on your process before an issue requires a tiebreaker. Agreeing on a tiebreaker early may help you build your conflict-resolution muscles so you'll be better armed for big decisions, such as adding another child or relocating—decisions that require knowledge across multiple domains, are hard to undo, and greatly affect the family as a whole.

Avoid Getting Stuck by Thinking Long Term

Another key ingredient in fighting the magnetic pull of equality is taking a longer-term view rather than judging things based on their current statuses, as is always tempting to do. Instead of locking in roles during the highly uncertain early days, the most effective entrepreneurs explicitly keep responsibilities and rewards fluid. They don't immediately shoot for equality in contributions because they realize that even if they could achieve balance now, that balance would soon change as the startup grows. Then, as the business evolves and they see how people contribute, they set up checkpoints in order to realign roles and rewards.

For the UpDown founding team, which wanted to develop a social network for investors, tensions were heightened by business-founder Michael's realization that he was contributing far more than technical-cofounder Phuc, even though they had agreed to an equal split of the ownership. Phuc had to point out that he couldn't develop their system until the other founders had solidified its requirements, and, as he explained to me, he also had to emphasize "the *long-run* contributions everyone would be making, even if during specific time periods, some founders [are] contributing more than others. . . . My tasks are the most important ones for getting the site launched and will be the most time consuming for quite a while!"

Going back to my student David, I would exhort him: If you are feeling the magnetic pull of equality, shoot for relative equality in the long run, while acknowledging that at any particular point in time you may be taking on more of the load, rather than having equality every step of the way. Don't keep score in the short term; instead, aim for overall parity in the long term. Support your partner through the tough days when she will least be able to contribute, because you will have your own dark days of imbalance during which she will be doing likewise for you. Avoid the pendulum effect of equal and opposite pain, discussed in the Chapter 7 story of Angela and her boyfriend with their back-and-forth job-change dynamic, by looking for collateral means of achieving balance and peace, even with one partner taking on a greater share of the load for a while.

In fact, Angela told me she discovered that, ultimately, her boyfriend wasn't necessarily demanding equal reciprocation; he just wanted "to see appreciation on my end for his effort." This is a recognition of equality's role as a means to an end and that appreciation can go a long way toward establishing an atmosphere of fairness.

Once you get into a long-term rhythm and a habit of showing appreciation for your partner's pitching in during your toughest days, you'll also find yourselves capable of taking advantage of more sophisticated approaches, such as the tag team used by dispersed founding teams and by couples who can arrange offsetting schedules.

Tag-Team

Geographical challenges often prompt entrepreneurs to come up with unusual solutions to management problems. I know of several startups with founders who are scattered between Silicon Valley and India or Israel, many times in different time zones. In some cases founders whose days are coming to an end hand off work to cofounders just as their day begins. For instance, the marketing team at online-workflow startup Zapier spread itself across Bangkok and four cities in three American time zones. Team member Matthew Guay writes: "We can hand off work to keep the wheels turning 24/7. I can write an article during the day in Bangkok, and my teammate Joe in Portland can edit it while I sleep. By the time I wake up, I've got corrections to work on."[20]

Similarly, ThirdPath Institute, a Philadelphia think tank, encourages dual-earner families to experiment with different approaches to childcare, such as creating complementary work schedules that allow parents to hand off primary childcare responsibilities to each other in a structured, foreseeable way.[21] My wife and I have a dual-income household and eight children. She is a doctor who is at the hospital for twenty-four hours when she is on call but is an extremely devoted mother and wife, and we struggled with how to balance our work obligations with taking care of our family. Hiring a nanny—"a third co-CEO for the family!"—seemed like a solution at first but quickly faltered when the nanny was sick or couldn't make it because of bad weather.

We figured that we needed a solution that was bigger than just one person, so we tried a day care center. Again, it seemed we had found our solution until the first time our youngest got sick and couldn't go to day care. Caught in a pinch, we put in a last-minute call to a temp agency. Next, we tried a "belt and suspenders" approach of having the kids in school and day care but also paying a nanny to be available in case of emergency, during school vacations, and the bookends of each day. My frugal wife cringed at the expense, but we were forced to accept this solution because of the inflexibility of her on-call schedule and my need to attend doctoral-program courses.

With the completion of my doctoral commitments (and with a much-compromised bank account), we finally settled on the ThirdPath approach of tag-teaming, both across days and within days. We began by analyzing which parts of each of our schedules were inflexible and tried to see if the other spouse could be flexible at those times. For my wife's on-call days, I made sure to be free to drop off the kids at school and pick them up and planned my schedule to be relatively flexible in case one of the kids got sick. When my schedule was inflexible—while teaching a class or when out of town on a business trip—my wife made sure to have a less rigid schedule. For example, on each of my teaching days, my last class ended at 1:00 p.m., so she started her patient appointments at about 1:15 in case we had to tag-team taking care of a sick child. On several occasions I walked straight from class to the school parking lot, where my wife had pulled her car next to mine to transfer a sleeping baby (with enough of a fever to stay out of day care). I could then take over caring for the sick baby for the rest of the afternoon while she saw patients at her office. We didn't want to adopt the Zapier marketing team's geographic dispersal—we usually prefer to have our family located on the same continent, if not under the same roof—but used offsetting schedules to accomplish the same tag-teaming goal. That system worked for us for more than a decade.

As you can see, I'm certainly not recommending that one spouse assume all economic responsibility while the other assumes all childcare and home maintenance. Instead, new parents need to be hyperaware of the common mistakes that most couples make: first expecting that the team will split childcare down the middle before the baby comes and then sliding into unconscious "triage" roles to get through sharply escalated postbirth responsibilities, with these triage roles eventually getting cast in stone, usually with much resentment. Instead of assuming that egalitarian prebaby arrangements will suffice, delve into what needs to happen and who does what. Which baby-specific tasks can only the mother do? Those go onto the mother's task list. Of the remaining tasks, which fit the father's capabilities and interests, and which would be relatively time consuming or draining for the mother to do? Those go onto the father's list. Are the to-do lists unbalanced? Now you can start trying to even things out by assigning the remaining tasks to the less-busy person. Most importantly, allow time and trial for your rhythm to develop. It was quite a while before my wife and I nailed down our tag-team method and learned how to keep it from being disrupted by occasional illnesses (and Boston blizzards).

The good news is that leveraging your natural inclinations can help you combat the bias for equality. Each spouse can identify the tasks for which he or she is a control-oriented "alpha." One spouse cares more about managing bill paying and finances, while the other is eager to decide about childcare. With the decision-making power comes also the burden of greater work in the area, but as long as the total efforts are roughly equal over long periods of time across work and home life, the arrangement can work well.

Daily Demands, Lifelong Commitments

Have you ever felt that you've overcontributed at home or at work? Perhaps you're feeling underappreciated at this very moment. Several of my students have come to me, both in entrepreneurial and personal situations, in this very bind. In these cases, my advice is to play the long game. Entrepreneurs build companies over a decade or more. A technical founder may contribute heavily to building out a product for a year while the sales-oriented founder has nothing to do. Just twelve months later, however, the roles could be reversed. Personal relationships require an even longer horizon. Five years' worth of heavy child rearing from one spouse could be followed by a decade of elder care from the other. By shifting our focus from what's fair *right this instant* to considering whether the household's—or company's—broad needs are being met over the longer term, we can help fight the bias toward equality that drives so much short-term, often unnecessary, conflict.

The overall lesson is that it pays to pause and step back from the day's immediate conflicts and take a longer view. It's a lesson from founders that we learn, in one form or another, throughout this book. It thus seems appropriate to conclude with a look at one more test—perhaps the ultimate test—of effective entrepreneurs' abilities to apply rational but counterintuitive thinking to complex, difficult situations: the battle between kingdom and throne.

CONCLUSION

I'VE SPENT ALMOST TWO DECADES studying the choices that entrepreneurs face as they get their businesses up and running. Over the course of my academic career, one key tension has kept reappearing and even became the underlying theme of my book *The Founder's Dilemmas: Anticipating and Avoiding the Pitfalls That Can Sink a Startup* and of the Founder's Dilemmas course I've taught at Harvard Business School, Stanford Engineering, and now at the University of Southern California. That tension is between wanting to be rich and wanting to be king. Nearly all entrepreneurs face this tension, most of them at multiple points in the evolution of their companies. Do they subordinate their desire for managerial control—to remain king—in order to ensure their businesses' greatest possible success and, ultimately, maximize their own wealth, becoming rich in the process? Or do they insist on continuing to remain king of their companies, despite the likelihood of growing a less-valuable entity?

Rich *and* king—founding and building a large and successful company while remaining in control throughout—is rarely a realistic option.[1] You can't expect first-rate business decisions from an executive committee and board that you've packed with loyalists, full commitment from a cofounder with whom you refuse to share decision-making control, and top quality from hires you micromanage.[2] Hence the biting tension of having to trade off one to increase the chances of achieving the other.

My appreciation for the importance of this trade-off has only deepened as I've continued to study entrepreneurs. They have to grapple with it when they are deciding when to become founders, whether to found alone or to attract the best cofounders, whether to self-finance or take outside investor money, how to build a board of directors, and at many other crossroads in the founding journey, including many of the ones I examine in this book. Most centrally, they have to grapple with it when they are deciding whether to remain on the CEO throne or to hand over the reins to someone who can grow a larger kingdom.

Giving up control of the baby you birthed and have raised for several years triggers a visceral heart reaction that can completely crowd out anything the head is saying or hearing. When founders' boards of directors tell them to give up the reins, founders use language like "being hit by a ton of bricks" or, as Jack Dorsey said when he was replaced as CEO of Twitter, receiving "a punch in the stomach."[3] In circumstances like these, entrepreneurs are no different from the rest of us in struggling mightily to overcome their emotions and apply rational thinking.

We face similar shocks when we realize that in many walks of life, the "You can do whatever you set your mind to do" advice that we've heard since childhood works better as an inspirational tool than as a depiction of reality. Our "both/and" aspirations often run smack into trade-offs we face across a wide range of professional and personal decisions.

For founders, powerful control tendencies can bring down even the highest potential of companies, as they did for Dean Kamen. On the flip side, a founder's drive and dedication to growing the company can lead to his giving up the throne, as it did for Lew Cirne. Let's delve into their journeys and then apply the patterns to our own journeys.

RICH VERSUS KING IN STARTUPS

Almost without exception, entrepreneurs start out wanting to do it all: to captain a high-impact, valuable company throughout its life, even as first-time founders. Sometimes an entrepreneur's desire to be both rich and king arises from his or her confidence that the business concept itself seems so powerful and ground breaking that letting go of it in any way would be unthinkable. "I am the one with the vision, so I have to be the one to bring it to reality! No one else will be able to build this as well as I can!" That's what happened to Dean Kamen.

Kamen was a brilliant, visionary inventor who wanted to change the world and fervently believed that engineers and scientists should be cultural icons on par with rock musicians and professional athletes. He was already an experienced—and very well remunerated—entrepreneur in the world of medical and robotics inventions. Then, inspired by a near-fall in the shower, Kamen and engineers at his firm came up with what came to be known as the Segway transporter but was originally named Ginger (after the great dancer Ginger Rogers). The concept of a self-balancing personal vehicle seemed a world-changing idea—not only to Kamen but to numerous experts like Steve Jobs and legendary venture capitalist John Doerr, who predicted that Ginger would reach $1 billion in sales faster than any new company ever. Kamen was enamored with the vehicle, envisioning entire cities built around the vehicle and seeing it as the best solution to pollution and traffic congestion.

Recognizing its potential, rather than license out this idea as he had done with his firm's past inventions, Kamen decided to form a company to develop and manufacture it. "We've decided to be the captain of our own soul and do Ginger ourselves," he said.[4] He also brought in senior executives to round out his team. His most senior hire was Tim Adams, the president of Chrysler Europe, as CEO. Kamen said that he needed someone like Adams to run the business so he could "get back to the fun stuff, inventing and engineering." He assured Adams that he "had no interest in being involved with manufacturing and all of those production details."[5]

However, the two were soon at odds with each other. When Adams made a decision about suppliers or manufacturing—his strong suits and Kamen's holes—Kamen overruled him. When an outsider wanted to see Ginger, company owner Kamen had to clear it; even CEO Adams did not have the power to do so. Kamen developed a disdain for Adams, saying, "He's not nearly as bright as most of the engineers I have, even though I pay him two or three times as much as any of them."[6] Soon after, Kamen replaced Adams with another CEO, only to fire the new CEO a year later. Things became quite draining for Kamen as he fought to keep control of his vision and company. Speaking to his employees, he said, "My idea of a good partner for Ginger is someone who leaves us in total control. We've spent a few million this year waiting for the right partner. . . . Imagine what life will be like when we can fund internal projects, and I can eat and sleep again."[7]

Over the opening decade of Segway's life, the company went through nearly one new CEO each year—a total of nine CEOs in those ten years—as Kamen insisted on retaining control of every key decision. This most high-potential of companies raised $176 million from investors but was worth only $10 million when it was eventually sold in 2009, going down in history as one of the biggest squanderers of potential ever.

Few of us paint our envisioned masterpieces on as public a canvas as Kamen's, but we too get passionate about painting them and believe that we should have the paintbrush in our own hands, regardless of our skill at handling it.

In doing so, we underestimate the fact that, in becoming real products, inventions have to adapt to markets, sometimes radically. Likewise for how startups change in the process of becoming real companies. Even for startups whose initial product-development process was smooth, company building introduces many challenges for which founders aren't ready. The company needs to change, often very quickly. As we saw with Dean Kamen, the product's inventor isn't usually the person best suited to guide the company through those changes, and a founder's remaining on the throne tends to result in a less valuable kingdom.

As I discovered when I studied 6,130 American ventures, when a founder retains strong control of the company, the harm to company value tends to become significant after two to three years. Before then, the founder's skills—whether rooted in technology, science, or the industry—are critical for helping get the startup off the ground in the development of its initial product. However, once the product is ready to be sold, the challenges of building a complex company usually eclipse the founder's skill set. The founder who never had to make a sales call now has to buy a suit to call on his first potential customer and then has to interview sales people, manage a team of them, and structure their compensation. And that's in just one of the new functions that have to be added! Founders who remain in control of their startups harm company value by an average of 17–22 percent, and the impact gets stronger each year.[8]

Lew Cirne, who built the enterprise software company Wily Technologies, felt these ramifications acutely. By the time the company was ready to ship version 2 of its product, Cirne was convinced that his rich-and-king vision was coming true: Customers were satisfied, sales were ramping up, and the team was working well together. He was in the process of raising his third round of financing, excited about bringing on the rocket fuel needed to power the rocket that Wily had become. Then his investors, who now controlled three of the five seats on Wily's board of directors, decided to replace him as CEO. He was shocked. He told me: "All I could think was: 'Where have I messed up? What have I been doing so wrong?'"

The investors decided that the company needed a leader whose skills were geared to its next stage. Cirne, an ace techie, lacked experience in the other business functions whose importance was skyrocketing. It was precisely because of his success at growing Wily quickly that he was replaced as CEO. In this paradox of entrepreneurial success, his success at building a rocket ship had hastened his demise as its CEO.

What happened to Lew Cirne happens to many of the most successful founders. In startups raising their third round of financing—a milestone only the most successful are able to achieve—fully half of founder-CEOs have been replaced, with three quarters of them forced out and the remainder voluntarily abdicating. These statistics come as a shock to most founders, who believe that success will merely reinforce their qualifications as CEO.[9]

However, the rich versus king tension isn't just a startup phenomenon. It occurs in many walks of life.

RICH VERSUS KING IN LIFE

When facing *career decisions*, many of us are like first-time entrepreneurs. We are convinced that with hard work, we can end up as power-wielding executives with impressive salaries at top companies, rich kings of the corporate world. We don't realize that instead we will probably face trade-offs requiring us to prioritize. If we want autonomy, we might have to settle on an option that doesn't pay well. Or, if it's money that drives us, we might have to forfeit some autonomy to get it. You've been trying to build a career as a brooding singer-songwriter, but no one notices you until you post a catchy little pop tune online. It gets tens of thousands of hits, major artists start remixing it, and an international record label offers to back you. But the label isn't interested in your brooding ballads. It wants the pop singer that you never intended to be. (The label also reminds you that if you refuse its offer, thousands of would-be artists are just waiting to take your place.) You can have success, but you'll have to give up trying to express the real you. The world can surprise us with unexpected options, which is great, but as often as not the options turn out to be mutually exclusive. They require tough choices.

Something similar can be said for *leadership trade-offs* within community activities or project teams. Control-oriented micromanagers may be able to perfectly execute projects if they do everything themselves. But in taking this approach, they are unable to complete as many activities and complete tasks much more slowly. Those who do delegate effectively build a bigger group with more hands on deck to complete more tasks, but they lose the ability to direct all realms. They have to give up some control while having to trust capable lieutenants to execute strategy.

In the *artistic or academic realms*, if you have always dreamed of writing a book or article, you may be able to accomplish it yourself. However, by involving a coauthor, you might end up with a better product and an increased chance of getting published. For instance, a colleague of mine had worked for a long time on an academic article that was continually rejected by top journals. It was clear that if he wanted to have a shot at acceptance, he should bring aboard a coauthor with deeper econometric skills. My colleague's choice came down to being the absolute king of a less-prestigious paper or sharing the prestige on a top-journal paper. This trade-off is a common one, as coauthored academic papers tend to be cited more often than those with solo authors.[10] (Guess I should have found a coauthor for this book!)

These trade-offs also arise in *marriage*. Those who value a high degree of control in their married lives—who want, say, finances to be done a certain way—will likely pay for that control by putting in the extra hours required to balance the checkbook and manage the accounts. When one spouse is more easy going and allows the control-oriented spouse to do the work, it can seem like one spouse is free-riding on the other's work. This can cause tensions to flare.

While the world of startups provides plenty of wrenching examples of failure in this area, it also offers guidance for how to navigate trade-offs effectively.

FINDING SOLUTIONS

As we've seen, the most successful entrepreneurs are those who are capable of identifying the emotional aspects of turning points and preventing those emotional aspects from dominating. They achieve this by gaining perspective on the trade-offs and on themselves, perspective that is particularly hard to achieve while being so focused on bringing an idea to fruition.

Achieve Separation

In the end, Lew Cirne of Wily Technology became an exemplar of how to deal with the rich versus king turning point—despite being blindsided initially. Like countless others, Cirne had spent years thinking of his startup as fused with himself. To a founder, 100 percent identification with the business is usually crucial to getting it off the ground, but the most enlightened founders see the necessity of prioritizing whatever is best for the venture and subordinating their desire to be boss.

Although Cirne's awakening didn't come until it was forced on him, ultimately he acknowledged that hanging onto the CEO job could significantly harm Wily and gave up the reins to a new CEO. He was left without a real role in the company. Wily went on to grow significantly and was eventually bought by Computer Associates for $375 million. Cirne, as he explained to me, was clear-eyed about the transition: He estimated that had he fought to remain king, the company would have been about one sixth as valuable as it ended up being.

Subordinating the "my" is one of life's biggest challenges, regardless of what it is in reference to. How many times have statements such as "My team doesn't follow directions" or "My company let me down" revealed an unhealthy identification with a project or organization? How many marriages have dissolved with one partner complaining, "This is not what I had envisioned for *my* marriage"?

Take a cue from Lew Cirne and recognize that the phrase "my baby" consists of two distinct words: "my" and "baby." Real parental devotion sometimes demands that you step back from "my" and do what's best for baby. Yet, as Lew Cirne discovered, in the long run what's best for baby may also be what's best for the parent, even if we can't see that at the time.

Keep Your Eye on the Long Term

Another lesson Cirne learned was to keep looking at the distant horizon, even when the day-to-day was urgent. He realized that Wily was only the first of many stops in a long entrepreneurial journey. In his next startup, New Relic (significantly, the name is an anagram of his own), he was able to have far more negotiating leverage with investors because if they didn't give him the terms he wanted, he could self-fund the company using his Wily winnings. He created startups in which he could make "rich" decisions in his first venture and then "king" decisions in his second so that in the long run he could achieve his goal of becoming rich and king.

We shouldn't overextend this prescription to parenting, in which the last thing we should be saying is, "If raising this kid doesn't work out, we can try something else with the next one." However, we can apply elements of Cirne's strategy to other personal relationships. When in the early stages of a long re-lationship or an intimate partnership, don't try to control every step. There will be weeks, months, and years when things feel out of balance—when your partner's situation is significantly better than yours, for example, or vice versa. While your wife is doing four years of medical residency and needing you to take more control, don't expect her to be an "equal" partner in the marriage, but realize that you might eventually decide to do a time-consuming PhD yourself and thus need to surrender control to her.

Often there's no practical way to achieve short-term balance. Better to view balance as a long-term goal. Relationships need to accommodate both people's needs but not necessarily at the same time.

Build Self-Awareness

Self-aware entrepreneurs prepare most effectively for the rich-versus-king wa-tershed. It was self-awareness that eventually helped Cirne yield to his investors at Wily and structure his next company differently. Indeed, self-awareness is the key to figuring out all kinds of trade-offs. Do we fully understand our motiva-tions? Do we know which potential outcomes we would celebrate and which we would regret? Do we see clearly which decisions at each step of the way lead to which outcomes?

If you're not aware of the frameworks that guide your life, it's easier than you might expect to make choices that don't fit with your deepest desires. Many people, including many of my students, answer "What should I do with my life?" with what their parents did or what their peers do, leaving them with a significant departure from their own key values.

As I approached college graduation, my wife was pregnant with our first child, but I was keen to try my hand at management consulting. I walked into an interview with the prominent McKinsey and Co. consulting firm, ready to convince them to hire me. I had also decided to be transparent with them about my constraints on the family side. I didn't want to travel much, and because I observed the Jewish Sabbath, I would not be able to work from sundown Fri-day until Saturday night. Surely, I thought, I could have my intellectual chal-lenge while founding my family and staying off of e-mail every Saturday! When the interviewer saw my yarmulke and heard about my three-month-old, his frank guidance was, "Don't even think about going into consulting."

That ended my one and only McKinsey interview! Instead, I was able to find a much smaller (and much less prestigious) consulting firm that had a lot of local clients to which I could be assigned. The firm was willing to accommodate my constraints and ended up being a much better fit for my entrepreneurial inclinations. *Gam zu l'tova!*

We all have dreams about how we want to make an impact on the world while living a satisfying life. However, realizing our dreams requires surmounting barriers that we often don't anticipate. The lessons we have learned from founders can increase the likelihood of our anticipating those barriers and thus making our dreams a reality. Rather than allowing yourself to be forced into a change, envision where you want to go ahead of time, assess when your passion or caution will become a barrier, anticipate how to harness failure and plan for success, and position yourself to build a wonderful life.

ACKNOWLEDGMENTS

Though we may think of high-impact startups as solo-founded, a deeper look reveals that getting a venture off the ground almost always requires a committed team. Bill Gates needed Paul Allen, Steve Jobs needed Steve Wozniak, Ben needed Jerry. So too with a book. Thanks go to the team who brought this book to life. At the top of my list, I thank all of my students for educating *me* about many of the issues and stories here. As R' Tarfon said in the Talmud (Ta'anit 7a) more than a millennium and a half ago, "I have learned much wisdom from my teachers, more from my colleagues, and the most from my students." I thank my teachers (and rebbeim) for helping shape the lenses and knowledge base that I bring to the issues tackled in this book and to my own research and teaching. I thank my USC colleagues for being so welcoming and collaborative during my initial years at Marshall and Greif. And I thank my prior mentors and colleagues for providing my early academic home and direction and for forcing me to climb out of a comfortable rut (see Chapter 4) to take on higher-impact roles in new arenas. As always, it was *gam zu l'tova.*

Margo Fleming persisted through disappointment a decade ago to bring this book under the Stanford banner—alas, only to leave me a publishing orphan when she moved on to a new career. I wish Margo v2.0 the best of luck! I owe thanks to Olivia Bartz for her delightful mix of cheerleading and critiquing throughout the writing and revising stages and to Steve Catalano for adopting this orphan and taking the parental reins during the last stages of the process. Thanks also go to Teresa Amabile for connecting me with Christy Fletcher (and to Eric Ries for helping sell me on Christy), to Christy for connecting me with Sylvie Greenberg, and to both Christy and Sylvie for sage guidance and moral support throughout the proposal and writing stages.

Andy O'Connell's gifted hands and Mac laptop have left a mark on almost every page of this book. Nita Prasad was a key thought partner during the early conceptual stages and a key pair of fresh eyes during the later stages of revising.

Daniel Doktori served as the first voice of the book critic, a role at which he excels, and Matt Holzapfel and Winnie Yu contributed incisive critiques of (and personal stories that helped shape) the emerging book proposal. Jordana Valencia took time away from her wedding and honeymoon (which finalized her claim to fame as part of a Founder's Dilemmas couple) to contribute personal vignettes, critiques, and cheerleading. I thank Dilip Rao for his overall inspiration and his gripping story and Angela Zhou and Rebecca Calman for their insightful contributions, both in class and outside as I sought to fill gaps in a couple of sections. I also thank my case protagonists and the gifted founders whose stories and openness helped enrich every chapter and every lesson.

I am grateful to Chana for letting me teach three thousand miles away from where I pick up my mail and for being the best cofounder of life that anyone could have or could wish for. I thank Talya, Tamar, Yair, Liat, Naava, Avital, Yishai, and Ahuva for being the best early hires into our Wasserman venture, and Sender, Chaim, and Shifra for joining the team to play starring roles in recent years. Thanks go to my parents for giving me the foundation on which everything has been built; for giving me the chance to enjoy daily salmon dinners, minyanim, and shiurim with them after three decades away; and for generously hosting me at 1153 for years on end and at 1138 for months on end. And I thank my parents-in-law for being among the earliest believers in the concept of this book and for the patriarchal and matriarchal roles you play for all generations of the family. May Hakadosh Baruch Hu enable them all to merit continuing to contribute to our families and communities until 120.

NOTES

CHAPTER 1

1. There is an interesting parallel here to founder compensation. Having experienced the power of handcuffs to deter them from leaving their employers, entrepreneurs themselves become prominent users of golden handcuffs for their own employees. They try to prevent their hires from leaving to pursue a shinier gem by forcing their employees to vest their equity by earning it over time as long as they remain at the company. In my data set of more than twenty thousand nonfounding startup executives, 99 percent of those hires had some form of vesting, with a full 82 percent having four or more years' worth of golden handcuffs. The startups' goal in using them: "You can check out any time, but you can never leave," at least for nearly half a decade.

2. Researchers Jennifer Merluzzi and Damon Phillips focused on MBA students pursuing an investment-banking career by working in the industry before coming back to school, joining the investment banking club and taking courses to reinforce that career, and doing a summer internship in that industry. They found that such "focused" students received fewer job offers and significantly lower compensation offers than students whose backgrounds were less focused on investment banking. See Merluzzi and Phillips 2015.

3. Wang and Murnighan 2013.

4. Most technicians began their careers after high school and so were still quite young.

5. Rawlinson 1978.

6. Sundaram and Yermack 2007.

7. Stross 2013, 12.

8. Becker 1960.

9. For instance, positive urgency (sparked by extreme positive emotions) and negative urgency (sparked by extreme negative emotions) can both lead to rash actions. For more details, see Cyders and Smith 2008.

10. Katz, n.d.

11. Wolfinger 2015.

12. Camerer and Lovallo 1999; Cooper, Woo, and Dunkelberg 1988.

13. Gimlet 2017a.

14. Cooper, Woo, and Dunkelberg 1988.

15. Sharot 2011, R942.

16. Sharot 2011, R943.

17. Walton 2016.

18. Experian 2016.

CHAPTER 2

1. Schoenberger 2015.

2. Kutz 2016.

3. Gillen et al. 2014.

4. Ries 2011.

5. Gompers 1995.

6. Ries 2011. See also the groundbreaking Blank 2005.

7. National Museum of American History, n.d.

8. Wozniak 2006, 122, 143.

9. Wozniak 2006, 122.

10. Wozniak 2006, 172.

11. Wozniak 2006, 177.

12. Hattiangadi, Medvec, and Gilovich 1995.

13. Wasserman and Galper 2008, 7.

14. Wasserman and Galper 2008, 6.

15. Toft-Kehler and Wennberg 2011.

16. Raffiee and Feng 2014.

17. Schwartz 2004.

18. Kowitt 2010.

19. Peterson 2016.

20. Quoted in Bernstein 2014. Similarly, psychologist Sheena Iyengar found that people are more likely to buy specific types of foods and to be more satisfied with their selections if they were presented with a moderate number of choices than if they had many choices. See Iyengar and Lepper 2000.

21. Dush, Cohan, and Amato 2003.

22. Sharot 2011, R944.

23. Wilkinson 2015.

24. Gallagher 2015.

25. Strasser and Becklund 1991.

26. Moore 2006.

27. Damasio 1994.

CHAPTER 3

1. Taleb 2012.

2. Gimlet 2014.

3. Zimmerman 2015.

4. Gimlet 2014.

5. Gimlet 2014.

6. Gimlet 2014.

7. Kay 2016.

8. Gimlet 2017b.

9. Gimlet 2017b.

10. Kelley, Singer, and Herrington 2011. The percentages of people who said that fear of failure would prevent them from setting up a business were as follows: in factor-driven economies, 37.3 percent; in efficiency-driven economies, 32.1 percent; in innovation-driven economies, 38.1 percent.

11. Knudson 2014.

12. Compton 2016.

13. Kahneman and Tversky 1979.

14. Churchill 1942.

15. Egan et al. 2013.

16. Fernald 2017.

17. Peter 1969.

18. Brunner 2017; Wiener-Bronner and Alesci 2017.

19. Ulukaya 2013.

20. Ulukaya 2013.

21. Ulukaya 2013.

22. Gasparro 2015.

23. Wasserman 2008.

24. Strasser and Becklund 1991, 333–334.

25. Orzeck 2015.

CHAPTER 4

1. The commercial is available at https://www.youtube.com/watch?v=45mMioJ5szc.

2. Sparks 2013.

3. This story comes from the Babylonian Talmud, Tractate Berachot, page 60b. The phrase "Gam zu l'tova" itself was originated by a sage named Nachum Ish Gamzu (described in Tractate Taanit, page 21a).

4. Warner 2017.

5. Warner 2017.

6. Wasserman and Galper 2008, 5.

7. Wasserman and Galper 2008.

8. Elkhorne 1967, 52.

9. Sperry 2012.

10. John, John, and Musser 1978, 100.

11. John, John, and Musser 1978.

12. John, John, and Musser 1978, 107.

13. John, John, and Musser 1978, 131. The situation was even more impossible than Tommy John remembered, for Sarah was actually eighty-nine years old. Abraham was ninety-nine when he received that promise of a child (Genesis 17:15–21 Art Scroll Chumash).

14. John, John, and Musser 1978, 125.

15. John, John, and Musser 1978, 126.

16. John, John, and Musser 1978, 152.

17. Simon 2010.

18. Tamir, Mitchell, and Gross 2008.

19. Seligman 1991.

20. Seligman 1991.

21. Dweck 2006.

22. Dowd and Mcafee 2015.

23. Sandberg 2016. She also described advice that helped her move on to her new state of life: "A few weeks after Dave died, I was talking to my friend Phil about a father-son activity that Dave was not here to do. We came up with a plan to fill in for Dave. I cried to him, 'But I want Dave.' Phil put his arm around me and said, 'Option A is not available. So let's just kick the [heck] out of option B.'" For more on this story, see Sandberg and Grant 2017.

24. Sandberg 2016.

25. Seligman 2004.

26. Sarkis 2012.

27. Hornik 2005.

28. Kahneman and Tversky 1979.

29. Gabbi Cahane, angel investor and chairman of the consultancy company Multiple, drove home this point in an interview with the *Financial Times*: "The right time for an entrepreneur to pack up and start the next thing is when they cross the admittedly thin line between relentless optimism and self delusion. This is extremely hard to gauge from the inside, so it's crucial that the founder establishes milestones, metrics and timelines to act as the arbiter of truth. Unless clear indicators are in place to translate what could be a hit from what is just hope, the entrepreneur will be driving blind. The harsh reality is that [sales, sign-ups, downloads] speak louder than words." Quoted in Newton 2016.

30. Wasserman 2004.

31. Wasserman 2004.

32. Taleb 2012.

33. Taleb 2012, 72.

34. Shin and Milkman 2016.

35. Gasparro 2015.

36. Erker and Thomas 2010.

37. Wasserman 2012.

38. Wilson and Gilbert 2003.

39. Gilbert et al. 1998.

40. Gilbert et al. 1998, 617.

41. Lublin 2016.

42. Fisher 2015.

43. Erker and Thomas 2010.

CHAPTER 5

1. Sandlin 2015.

2. Sandlin 2015.

3. The original application of the term "blueprints" to entrepreneurial decision making came from the Stanford Project on Emerging Companies (SPEC) and its analyses of the handful of core models used instinctively by founders to build their organizations. For more on this, see Baron and Hannan 2002. However, SPEC did not delve into the specific origins of or influences on founders' blueprints or the process by which founders faced disconnects between their personal blueprints and the demands of the startup, as we explore here.

4. Sandlin 2015.

5. Wasserman, Bussgang, and Gordon 2010.

6. Wasserman, Bussgang, and Gordon 2010, 2–3.

7. Schwartz 2012.

8. Groysberg 2010.

9. Hamori 2010.

10. Useem 2012.

11. Indy_dad 2012.

12. Cathies 2012.

13. Hendrix 2007.

14. Kahneman 2013.

15. McPherson, Smith-Lovin, and Cook 2001.

16. McPherson, Smith-Lovin, and Cook 2001.

17. Nahemow and Lawton 1975.

18. Shenker 1972, 33.

19. For more information on this collaboration, the Cooperative Congressional Election Study (CCES), see https://cces.gov.harvard.edu/pages/welcome-cooperative -congressional-election-study.

20. Butters and Hare 2017.

21. Mitchell et al. 2014.

22. Youyou et al. 2017.

23. Blackwell and Lichter 2005. Because of the small sample size, they dropped women of Asian, American Indian, Eskimo, and Aleut descent.

24. Ruef, Aldrich, and Carter 2003.

25. Lunden 2017.

26. Sumagaysay 2015.

27. Snap 2017.

28. Gompers, Mukharlyamov, and Xuan 2016.

29. Gompers, Mukharlyamov, and Xuan 2016, 628.

30. Gompers, Mukharlyamov, and Xuan 2016, 627.

31. Cubiks 2013. There were approximately five hundred responses to the survey from people in fifty-four different countries: 63 percent from Europe, 26 percent from Oceania, 8 percent from the United States, and 3 percent from Africa.

32. Rivera 2015.

33. Mark 2003.

34. McPherson, Smith-Lovin, and Cook 2001.

35. Umphress et al. 2007.

CHAPTER 6

1. Groysberg and Abrahams 2010.

2. Janisj 2012.

3. Gersick 1994, 25. Please note that Gersick used pseudonyms for the company name and the CEO's name.

4. Klein and Calderwood 1996.

5. Wasserman and Galper 2008.

6. Wasserman and Galper 2008.

7. Wasserman and Galper 2008.

8. Wasserman and Galper 2008.

9. Perlow 2003.

10. Gross and John 2003; Kashdan and Rottenberg 2010.

11. Kashdan and Rottenberg 2010, 871.

12. Neisser 1979.

13. Wasserman and Maurice 2008a, 2008b.

14. For the classic exploration of this phenomenon, see Granovetter 1973.

15. Wasserman and Maurice 2008a, 2008b.

16. Gawande's checklists focus on achieving greater safety, efficiency, and consistency, which are very different goals from ours here. See Gawande 2009.

17. Gompers, Mukharlyamov, and Xuan 2016.

18. Wasserman 2002.

19. Walters 2016.

20. Allmendinger, Hackman, and Lehman 1996.

21. For more on difficult conversations, see Stone, Heen, and Patton 2010.

22. Alter 2012.

23. Gottman, n.d. Gottman's research work with couples started in 1972 and continues today. To date, he has completed twelve studies with more than 3,000 couples. Gottman's divorce prediction research specifically included 677 couples.

24. Gottman, n.d.

25. Wasserman 2004.

26. Wasserman 2004.

27. Quoted in Lisitsa 2014.

28. Quoted in Radford 2004.

29. Radford 2004.

CHAPTER 7

1. Wasserman and Braid 2012. All information and quotations about ProLab in this section come from this source.

2. Dyer, Dyer, and Gardner 2012.

3. Wasserman and Marx 2008.

4. Wasserman 2012.

5. According to the National Federation of Independent Business, firms employing family members represent between 80 percent and 90 percent of firms worldwide, and firms that include both spouses represent about one-third of all family businesses. For more details, see Dyer, Dyer, and Gardner 2012.

6. Richard S. Tedlow, personal communication, June 2004.

7. Belmi and Pfeffer 2015.

8. For development of these different dimensions of difficult conversations and their application to the difficult conversations between health professionals and their patients, see Browning et al. 2007.

9. Keating et al. 2013.

10. Sanford 2003.

11. Mosendz 2016; Experian 2016. Perhaps most surprising, 20 percent of the men had secret financial accounts that they hadn't told their partners about. The same was true of 12 percent of the women.

12. Dezső and Loewenstein 2012, 996.

13. Krackhardt 1999.

14. Barmash 1988.

15. Forden 2001, 141.

16. See Wasserman 2012.

17. Krause, Priem, and Love 2015.

18. Krause, Priem, and Love 2015, 2099.

19. US Bureau of Labor Statistics 2014.

20. Szuchman and Anderson 2012, 10.

21. Szuchman and Anderson 2012, 11.

22. Rogers 2004. Marital happiness provides important context for marital stability: The odds of divorce are highest when spouses' resources are similar and marital happiness was at low or moderate levels.

23. Bass 2015.

24. Dienhart 2001.

CHAPTER 8

1. Wasserman and Braid 2012.

2. Wasserman and Braid 2012.

3. Wasserman and Braid 2012.

4. Lashinsky 2017, 78.

5. Javitch 2006.

6. Wasserman and Braid 2012.

7. Akalp 2015.

8. Wasserman and Braid 2012. All other information and quotations about ProLab in this section come from this source.

9. Wasserman and Braid 2012.

10. Wasserman and Braid 2012.

11. Javitch 2006.

12. Li 2016.

13. Keating et al. 2013.

14. Wasserman 2012. Among the 3,600 startups in my data set, 16 percent had been solo founded, 37 percent had two cofounders, 24 percent had three cofounders, and the remainder had four or more cofounders.

15. Wasserman 2012.

16. Hellmann and Wasserman 2016.

17. Keates 2015.

18. Wasserman and Maurice 2008a.

19. Wasserman 2012.

20. Guay, n.d.

21. Valcour 2015.

CONCLUSION

1. Wasserman 2017.

2. Wasserman 2012.

3. Kirkpatrick 2011.

4. Kemper 2003, 80.

5. Kemper 2003, 46.

6. Kemper 2003, 54.

7. Kemper 2003, 85.

8. Wasserman 2017.

9. Wasserman 2012.

10. Wuchty, Jones, and Uzzi 2007.

REFERENCES

Akalp, N. 2015. "Keepin' It in the Family: How to Structure a Business with Your Closest Relatives." *Entrepreneur*, April 6. https://www.entrepreneur.com/article/244249.

Allmendinger, J., R. Hackman, and E. Lehman. 1996. "Life and Work in Symphony Orchestras." *Musical Quarterly* 80 (2): 184–219.

Alter, J. 2012. "How We Fight—Cofounders in Love and War." *Steve Blank* (blog), October 21. https://steveblank.com/2012/10/21/how-we-fight-cofounders-in-love-and-war.

Barmash, I. 1988. "Gucci Family, Split by Feud, Sells Large Stake in Retailer." *New York Times*, June 8. http://www.nytimes.com/1988/06/08/business/gucci-family-split-by -feud-sells-large-stake-in-retailer.html.

Baron, J. N., and M. T. Hannan. 2002. "Organizational Blueprints for Success in High-Tech Start-Ups: Lessons from the Stanford Project on Emerging Companies." *California Management Review* 44 (3): 8–36.

Bass, B. C. 2015. "Preparing for Parenthood? Gender, Aspirations, and the Reproduction of Labor Market Inequality." *Gender and Society* 29 (June): 362–385.

Becker, H. S. 1960. "Notes on the Concept of Commitment." *American Journal of Sociology* 97:15–22.

Belmi, P., and J. Pfeffer. 2015. "How 'Organization' Can Weaken the Norm of Reciprocity: The Effects of Attributions for Favors and a Calculative Mindset." *Academy of Management Discoveries* 1 (1): 36–57.

Bernstein, E. 2014. "How You Make Decisions Says a Lot About How Happy You Are." *Wall Street Journal*, October 6. https://www.wsj.com/articles/how-you-make -decisions-says-a-lot-about-how-happy-you-are-1412614997.

Blackwell, D., and D. Lichter. 2005. "Homogamy Among Dating, Cohabiting, and Married Couples." *Sociological Quarterly* 45 (4): 719–737.

Blank, S. 2005. *The Four Steps to the Epiphany: Successful Strategies for Products That Win*. Palo Alto, CA: K&S Ranch Press.

Browning, D. M., E. C. Meyer, R. D. Truog, and M. Z. Solomon. 2007. "Difficult Conversations in Health Care: Cultivating Relational Learning to Address the Hidden Curriculum." *Academic Medicine—Philadelphia* 82 (9): 905.

Brunner, R. 2017. "How Chobani's Hamdi Ulukaya Is Winning America's Culture War." *Fast Company*, March 20. https://www.fastcompany.com/3068681/how-chobani -founder-hamdi-ulukaya-is-winning-americas-culture-war.

Butters, R., and C. Hare. 2017. "Three-Fourths of Americans Regularly Talk Politics Only with Members of Their Own Political Tribe." *Washington Post*, May 1. https://www.washingtonpost.com/news/monkey-cage/wp/2017/05/01/three-fourths-of-americans-regularly-talk-politics-only-with-members-of-their-own-political-tribe/.

Camerer, C., and D. Lovallo. 1999. "Overconfidence and Excess Entry: An Experimental Approach." *American Economic Review* 89 (1): 306–318.

Cathies. 2012. Untitled post. In "Driving on the Left . . . Easy Transition or Real Nightmare??" thread. *Fodor's Travel*, July 13. http://www.fodors.com/community/europe/driving-on-the-lefteasy-transition-or-real-nightmare.cfm.

Churchill, W. 1942. Speech in the House of Commons. November 11.

Compton, S. 2016. "Regrets." *Medium*. Previously available at https://medium.com/@stephcompton/regrets-5e19ca4d17fb.

Cooper, A. C., C. Y. Woo, and W. C. Dunkelberg. 1988. "Entrepreneurs' Perceived Chances for Success." *Journal of Business Venturing* 3:97–108.

Cubiks. 2013. "Cubiks International Survey on Job and Cultural Fit." July. https://www.learnvest.com/wp-content/uploads/2017/02/Cubiks-Survey-Results-July-2013.pdf.

Cyders, M. A., and G. T. Smith. 2008. "Emotion-Based Dispositions to Rash Action: Positive and Negative Urgency." *Psychological Bulletin* 134 (6): 807.

Damasio, A. R. 1994. *Descartes' Error: Emotion, Reason, and the Human Brain*. New York: Putnam.

Dezső, L., and G. Loewenstein. 2012. "Lenders' Blind Trust and Borrowers' Blind Spots: A Descriptive Investigation of Personal Loans." *Journal of Economic Psychology* 33 (5): 996–1011.

Dienhart, A. 2001. "Make Room for Daddy: The Pragmatic Potentials of a Tag-Team Structure for Parenting." *Journal of Family Issues* 22:973–999.

Dowd, K. E., and T. McAfee. 2015. "Sheryl Sandberg's Husband Died from Heart-Related Causes, *People* Learns." *People*, May 12. http://people.com/celebrity/sheryl-sandbergs-husband-dave-goldberg-died-from-heart-related-causes.

Dush, C. M. K., C. L. Cohan, and P. R. Amato. 2003. "The Relationship Between Cohabitation and Marital Quality and Stability: Change Across Cohorts?" *Journal of Marriage and Family* 65 (3): 539–549.

Dweck, C. S. 2006. *Mindset: The New Psychology of Success*. New York: Random House.

Dyer, W. G., W. J. Dyer, and R. G. Gardner. 2013. "Should My Spouse Be My Partner? Preliminary Evidence from the Panel Study of Income Dynamics." *Family Business Review* 26 (1): 68–80.

Egan, K., J. B. Lozano, S. Hurtado, and M. H. Case. 2013. *The American Freshman: National Norms Fall 2013*. Los Angeles: UCLA Higher Education Research Institute.

Elkhorne, J. L. 1967. "Edison—the Fabulous Drone." *73*, March, pp. 52–54.

Erker, S., and B. Thomas. 2010. "Finding the First Rung: A Study on the Challenges Facing Today's Frontline Leader." http://www.ddiworld.com/ddi/media/trend-research/findingthefirstrung_mis_ddi.pdf.

Experian. 2016. "Newlyweds and Credit: Survey Results." https://www.experian.com/blogs/ask-experian/newlyweds-and-credit-survey-results/.

Fernald, M., ed. 2017. "The State of the Nation's Housing, 2017." http://www.jchs.harvard.edu/sites/jchs.harvard.edu/files/harvard_jchs_state_of_the_nations_housing_2017.pdf.

Fisher, A. 2015. "Don't Let Yourself Get Pushed into a Job Promotion." *Fortune*, June 18. http://fortune.com/2015/06/18/job-promotion-mistakes/.

Forden, S. G. 2001. *The House of Gucci: A Sensational Story of Murder, Madness, Glamour, and Greed.* 4th ed. New York: William Morrow.

Gallagher, L. 2015. "The Education of Airbnb's Brian Chesky." *Fortune*, June 26. http://fortune.com/brian-chesky-airbnb.

Gasparro, A. 2015. "At Chobani, Rocky Road from Startup Status." *Wall Street Journal*, May 17. https://www.wsj.com/articles/at-chobani-rocky-road-from-startup-status-1431909152.

Gawande, A. 2009. *Checklist Manifesto.* New York: Metropolitan Books.

Gersick, C. J. G. 1994. "Pacing Strategic Change: The Case of a New Venture." *Academy of Management Journal* 37 (1): 9–45.

Gilbert, D. T., E. C. Pinel, T. D. Wilson, S. J. Blumberg, and T. P. Wheatley. 1998. "Immune Neglect: A Source of Durability Bias in Affective Forecasting." *Journal of Personality and Social Psychology* 75 (3): 617.

Gillen, J. B., M. E. Percival, L. E. Skelly, B. J. Martin, R. B. Tan, M. A. Tarnopolsky, and M. J. Gibala. 2014. "Three Minutes of All-Out Intermittent Exercise per Week Increases Skeletal Muscle Oxidative Capacity and Improves Cardiometabolic Health." *PLoS One* 9 (11). http://journals.plos.org/plosone/article?id=10.1371/journal.pone.0111489.

Gimlet. 2014. "Dating Ring of Fire." *StartUp Podcast*, season 2, episode 9. https://www.gimletmedia.com/startup/dating-ring-of-fire.

———. 2017a. "Friendster: Part 1." *StartUp Podcast*, season 5, episode 2. https://www.gimletmedia.com/startup/friendster-part-1-season-5-episode-2.

———. 2017b. "Life after Startup." *StartUp Podcast*, season 5, episode 7. https://www.gimletmedia.com/startup/life-after-startup-season-5-episode-7.

Gompers, P. 1995. "Optimal Investment, Monitoring, and the Staging of Venture Capital." *Journal of Finance* 50:1461–1489.

Gompers, P. A., V. Mukharlyamov, and Y. Xuan. 2016. "The Cost of Friendship." *Journal of Financial Economics* 119 (3): 626–644.

Gottman, J. n.d. "The Four Horsemen of the Apocalypse." *The Gottman Institute.* https://www.youtube.com/watch?v=1o30Ps-_8is.

Granovetter, M. 1973. "The Strength of Weak Ties." *American Journal of Sociology* 78:1360–1380.

Gross, J. J., and O. P. John. 2003. "Individual Differences in Two Emotion Regulation Processes: Implications for Affect, Relationships, and Well-Being." *Journal of Personality and Social Psychology* 85 (2): 348.

Groysberg, B. 2010. *Chasing Stars: The Myth of Talent and the Portability of Performance.* Princeton, NJ: Princeton University Press.

Groysberg, B., and R. Abrahams. 2010. "Managing Yourself: Five Ways to Bungle a Job Change." *Harvard Business Review*, January–February. https://hbr.org/2010/01/managing-yourself-five-ways-to-bungle-a-job-change.

Guay, M. n.d. "How to Work in Different Timezones." *Zapier.* https://zapier.com/learn/remote-work/remote-work-time-shift/ (accessed February 27, 2018).

Hamori, M. 2010. "Managing Yourself: Job-Hopping to the Top and Other Career Fallacies." *Harvard Business Review*, July–August. https://hbr.org/2010/07/managing-yourself-job-hopping-to-the-top-and-other-career-fallacies.

Hattiangadi, N., V. H. Medvec, and T. Gilovich. 1995. "Failing to Act: Regrets of Terman's Geniuses." *International Journal of Aging and Human Development* 40 (3): 175–185.

Hellmann, T., and N. Wasserman. 2016. "The First Deal: The Division of Founder Equity in New Ventures." *Management Science* 63 (8): 2647–2666.

Hendrix, H. 2007. *Getting the Love You Want: A Guide for Couples.* New York: Macmillan.

Hornik, D. 2005. "Pandora and Persistence." *VentureBlog*, September 7. http://www.ventureblog.com/2005/09/pandora-and-persistence.html.

Indy_dad. 2012. Untitled post. In "Driving on the Left . . . Easy Transition or Real Nightmare??" thread. *Fodor's Travel*, July 13. http://www.fodors.com/community/europe/driving-on-the-lefteasy-transition-or-real-nightmare.cfm.

Iyengar, S. S., and M. R. Lepper. 2000. "When Choice Is Demotivating: Can One Desire Too Much of a Good Thing?" *Journal of Personality and Social Psychology* 79 (6): 995.

Janisj. 2012. Untitled post. In "Driving on the Left . . . Easy Transition or Real Nightmare??" thread. *Fodor's Travel*, July 13. http://www.fodors.com/community/europe/driving-on-the-lefteasy-transition-or-real-nightmare.cfm

Javitch, D. G. 2006. "10 Tips for Working with Family Members." *Entrepreneur*, July 10. https://www.entrepreneur.com/article/159446.

John, T., S. John, and J. Musser. 1978. *The Tommy John Story.* Old Tappan, NJ: Fleming H. Revell.

Kahneman, D. 2013. *Thinking, Fast and Slow.* New York: Farrar, Straus and Giroux.

Kahneman, D., and A. Tversky. 1979. "Prospect Theory: An Analysis of Decision Under Risk." *Econometrica* 47 (2): 263–291.

Kashdan, T. B., and J. Rottenberg. 2010. "Psychological Flexibility as a Fundamental Aspect of Health." *Clinical Psychology Review* 30 (7): 865–878.

Katz, E. M. n.d. "Is Your Checklist Getting Too Long?" *Evan Marc Katz* (blog). https://www.evanmarckatz.com/blog/dating-tips-advice/is-your-checklist-getting-too-long (accessed February 27, 2018).

Kay, L. 2016. "Congratulations on Quitting without a Gameplan! (Seriously.)." *Medium*, August 15. https://medium.com/@laurenikay/congratulations-on-quitting-without-a-gameplan-seriously-6dbc3415e13d.

Keates, N. 2015. "The House That Saved Their Marriage." *Wall Street Journal*, July 16. https://www.wsj.com/articles/the-house-that-saved-their-marriage-1437054227.

Keating, D. M., J. C. Russell, J. Cornacchione, and S. W. Smith. 2013. "Family Communication Patterns and Difficult Family Conversations." *Journal of Applied Communication Research* 41 (2): 160–180.

Kelley, D. J., S. Singer, and M. Herrington. 2011. "Entrepreneurial Perceptions, Intentions and Societal Attitudes in 54 Economies." In "Global Entrepreneurship Monitor: 2011 Global Report," 7–9. https://www.slideshare.net/emprenupf/gem-2011.

Kemper, S. 2003. *Code Name Ginger*. Boston: Harvard Business School Press.

Kirkpatrick, D. 2011. "Twitter Was Act One." *Vanity Fair*, March 3. https://www.vanityfair.com/news/2011/04/jack-dorsey-201104.

Klein, G. A., and R. Calderwood. 1996. "Investigations of Naturalistic Decision Making and the Recognition-Primed Decision Model." Army Research Institute Research Note 96-43. http://www.au.af.mil/au/awc/awcgate/army/ari_natural_dm.pdf.

Knudson, T. 2014. "Why We All Have Fear of Failure." *Psych Central*. http://psychcentral.com/blog/archives/2014/06/23/why-we-all-have-fear-of-failure.

Kowitt, B. 2010. "Inside the Secret World of Trader Joe's." *Fortune*, August 23. http://fortune.com/2010/08/23/inside-the-secret-world-of-trader-joes/.

Krackhardt, D. 1999. "The Ties That Torture: Simmelian Tie Analysis in Organizations." *Research in the Sociology of Organizations* 16:183–210.

Krause, R., R. Priem, and L. Love. 2015. "Who's in Charge Here? Co-CEOs, Power Gaps, and Firm Performance." *Strategic Management Journal* 36 (13): 2099–2110.

Kutz, S. 2016. "Why NFL Player Ryan Broyles Lives Like He Made $60,000 Last Year, and Not $600,000." *MarketWatch*, January 31. http://www.marketwatch.com/story/nfl-player-ryan-broyles-has-made-millions-but-still-uses-groupon-2015-09-17.

Lashinsky, A. 2017. *Wild Ride: Inside Uber's Quest for World Domination*. New York: Portfolio.

Li, J. B. 2016. "On Single-Domain Role Transitions in Multiplex Relationships." Paper presented at Strategic Management Society conference, Hong Kong, December 10–12.

Lisitsa, E. 2014. "Self Care: The Four Horsemen." Gottman Institute. https://www.gottman.com/blog/self-care-the-four-horsemen.

Lublin, J. S. 2016. "How Companies Are Different When More Women Are in Power." *Wall Street Journal*, September 27. https://www.wsj.com/articles/how-companies-are-different-when-more-women-are-in-power-1474963802.

Lunden, I. 2017. "Snapchat Paid Reggie Brown $157.5M to Settle His 'Ousted Founder' Lawsuit." *TechCrunch*, February 2. https://techcrunch.com/2017/02/02/snapchat-reggie-brown/.

Mark, N. P. 2003. "Culture and Competition: Homophily and Distancing Explanations for Cultural Niches." *American Sociological Review* 68 (3): 319–345.

McPherson, M., L. Smith-Lovin, and J. Cook. 2001. "Birds of a Feather: Homophily in Social Networks." *Annual Review of Sociology* 27:415–444.

Merluzzi, J., and D. J. Phillips. 2015. "The Specialist Discount: Negative Returns for MBAs with Focused Profiles in Investment Banking." *Administrative Science Quarterly* 61 (1): 87–124.

Mitchell, A., J. Gottfried, J. Kiley, and K. E. Matsa. 2014. "Political Polarization and Media Habits." Pew Research Center, October 21. http://www.journalism.org/2014/10/21/political-polarization-media-habits/.

Moore, K. 2006. *Bowerman and the Men of Oregon: The Story of Oregon's Legendary Coach and Nike's Co-founder.* Emmaus, PA: Rodale.

Mosendz, P. 2016. "A Third of Newlyweds Are in the Dark About Their Spouse's Finances." *Chicago Tribune*, May 2. http://www.chicagotribune.com/business/ct-personal-finance-newlywed-money-20160502-story.html.

Nahemow, L., and M. Lawton. 1975. "Similarity and Propinquity in Friendship Formation." *Journal of Personality and Social Psychology* 32 (2): 205–213.

National Museum of American History. n.d. "Nike Waffle Trainer." http://americanhistory.si.edu/collections/search/object/nmah_1413776 (accessed May 4, 2018).

Neisser, U. 1979. "The Control of Information Pickup in Selective Looking." In *Perception and Its Development: A Tribute to Eleanor J Gibson*, edited by A. D. Pick, 201–219. Hillsdale, NJ: Lawrence Erlbaum.

Newton, R. 2016. "Start-Ups and the Founder's Dilemma." *Financial Times*, June 7. https://www.ft.com/content/11de999e-d4d5-11e5-829b-8564e7528e54.

Orzeck, K. 2015. "Chobani CEO's Deal with Ex-Wife in Ownership Spat OK'd." *Law360*, April 14. https://www.law360.com/articles/643365/chobani-ceo-s-deal-with-ex-wife-in-ownership-spat-ok-d.

Perlow, L. A. 2003. "When Silence Spells Trouble at Work." *Harvard Business School Working Knowledge*, May 26. https://hbswk.hbs.edu/item/when-silence-spells-trouble-at-work.

Peter, L. J., and R. Hull. 1969. *The Peter Principle.* London: Souvenir Press.

Peterson, H. 2016. "Whole Foods' New Stores Are Unrecognizable." *Business Insider*, April 28. http://uk.businessinsider.com/inside-whole-foods-new-365-stores-2016-4.

Radford, T. 2004. "Psychologist Says Maths Can Predict Chances of Divorce." *The Guardian*, February 13. https://www.theguardian.com/uk/2004/feb/13/science.research.

Raffiee, J., and J. Feng. 2014. "Should I Quit My Day Job? A Hybrid Path to Entrepreneurship." *Academy of Management Journal* 57 (4): 936–963.

Rawlinson, M. J. 1978. *Labour Turnover in the Technician and Equivalent Trades of the Royal Australian Air Force: An Economic Analysis.* Canberra, Australia: Department of Defense.

Ries, E. 2011. *The Lean Startup: How Today's Entrepreneurs Use Continuous Innovation to Create Radically Successful Businesses.* New York: Crown.

Rivera, L. 2015. "Guess Who Doesn't Fit in at Work." *New York Times*, May 30. https://www.nytimes.com/2015/05/31/opinion/sunday/guess-who-doesnt-fit-in-at-work.html.

Rogers, S. 2004. "Dollars, Dependency, and Divorce." *Journal of Marriage and Family* 66:59–74.

Ruef, M., H. E. Aldrich, and N. Carter. 2003. "The Structure of Founding Teams: Homophily, Strong Ties, and Isolation Among U.S. Entrepreneurs." *American Sociological Review* 68:195–222.

Sandberg, S. 2016. "It's the Hard Days That Determine Who You Are." *Boston Globe*, May 16. https://www.bostonglobe.com/opinion/2016/05/16/hard-days-that-determine -who-you-are/3R5MODlB8w8QcDt8X8BlEO/story.html.

Sandberg, S., and A. Grant. 2017. *Option B: Facing Adversity, Building Resilience, and Finding Joy*. New York: Knopf/Random House.

Sandlin, D. 2015. "The Backwards Brain Bicycle." *Smarter Every Day* 133. https://www .youtube.com/watch?v=MFzDaBzBlL0.

Sanford, K. 2003. "Problem-Solving Conversations in Marriage: Does It Matter What Topics Couples Discuss?" *Personal Relationships* 10 (1): 97–112.

Sarkis, S. 2012. "Quotes on Letting Go." *Psychology Today*, October 25. https://www .psychologytoday.com/us/blog/here-there-and-everywhere/201210/quotes-letting-go.

Schoenberger, C. R. 2015. "Want to Be an Entrepreneur? Beware of Student Debt." *Wall Street Journal*, May 26. https://www.wsj.com/articles/want-to-be-an-entrepreneur -beware-of-student-debt-1432318500.

Schwartz, B. 2004. *The Paradox of Choice: Why More Is Less*. New York: Ecco/Harper-Collins.

Schwartz, J. 2012. "End Game: Curt Schilling and the Destruction of 38 Studios." *Boston Magazine*, July 23. https://www.bostonmagazine.com/2012/07/23/38-studios-end -game.

Seligman, M. 1991. *Learned Optimism: How to Change Your Mind and Your Life*. New York: Pocket.

Seligman, M. E. 2004. *Authentic Happiness: Using the New Positive Psychology to Realize Your Potential for Lasting Fulfillment*. New York: Simon and Schuster.

Sharot, T. 2011. "The Optimism Bias." *Current Biology* 21 (23): R941–R945.

Shenker, I. 1972. "2 Critics Here Focus on Films as Language Conference Opens." *New York Times*, December 28, p. 33.

Shin, J., and K. L. Milkman. 2016. "How Backup Plans Can Harm Goal Pursuit: The Unexpected Downside of Being Prepared for Failure." *Organizational Behavior and Human Decision Processes* 135:1–9.

Simon, S. 2010. "Stephen Strasburg, Meet Tommy John." *NPR*, August 28. http://www .npr.org/templates/story/story.php?storyId=129492123.

Smart, G., and R. Street. 2008. *Who: The A Method for Hiring*. New York: Random House.

Snap. 2017. "Snap, Inc.: Form S-1 Registration Statement." U.S. Securities and Exchange Commission, February 2. https://www.sec.gov/Archives/edgar/data/1564408/ 000119312517029199/d270216ds1.htm.

Sparks, A. 2013. "Losing a Battle, and Focusing on Winning the War—Part 1." *Medium*. https://medium.com/@sparkszilla/losing-a-battle-and-focusing-on-winning-the -war-part-i-6369b8bf9d24.

Sperry, T. 2012. "Tommy John Accepts Role in Baseball and Medical History." *CNN*, April 24. http://www.cnn.com/2012/04/24/health/tommy-john-surgery/.

Stone, D., S. Heen, and B. Patton. 2010. *Difficult Conversations: How to Discuss What Matters Most*. New York: Penguin.

Strasser, J. B., and L. Becklund. 1991. *Swoosh: The Unauthorized Story of Nike and the Men Who Played There.* New York: Harcourt Brace Jovanovich.

Stross, R. 2013. *The Launch Pad: Inside Y Combinator.* New York: Penguin.

Sumagaysay, L. 2013. "Quoted: On Snapchat, Startup Drama and 'Lawyering Up.'" *Silicon Beat,* December 12. http://www.siliconbeat.com/2013/12/12/quoted-on -snapchat-startup-drama-and-lawyering-up/.

Sundaram, R., and D. Yermack. 2007. "Pay Me Later: Inside Debt and Its Role in Managerial Compensation." *Journal of Finance* 62 (4): 1551–1588.

Szuchman, P., and J. Anderson. 2012. *It's Not You, It's the Dishes: How to Minimize Conflict and Maximize Happiness in Your Relationship.* New York: Random House.

Taleb, N. N. 2012. *Antifragile: Things That Gain from Disorder.* New York: Random House.

Tamir, M., C. Mitchell, and J. J. Gross. 2008. "Hedonic and Instrumental Motives in Anger Regulation." *Psychological Science* 19 (4): 324–328.

Toft-Kehler, R. V., and K. Wennberg. 2011. "Barriers to Learning in Entrepreneurship." Paper presented at Academy of Management Annual Meeting, San Antonio, TX, August 12–16.

Ulukaya, H. 2013. "Chobani's Founder on Growing a Start-Up Without Outside Investors." *Harvard Business Review,* October. https://hbr.org/2013/10/chobanis-founder -on-growing-a-start-up-without-outside-investors.

Umphress, E., K. Smith-Crowe, A., Brief, J., Dietz, and M. Watkins. 2007. "When Birds of a Feather Flock Together and When They Do Not." *Journal of Applied Psychology* 92 (2): 396–409.

US Bureau of Labor Statistics. 2014. "Women in the Labor Force: A Databook." https:// www.bls.gov/cps/wlf-databook-2013.pdf.

Useem, J. 2002. "[3M] + [General Electric] = ?" *Fortune,* August 12. http://archive .fortune.com/magazines/fortune/fortune_archive/2002/08/12/327038/index.htm.

Valcour, M. 2015. "Navigating Tradeoffs in a Dual-Career Marriage." *Harvard Business Review,* April 14. https://hbr.org/2015/04/navigating-tradeoffs-in-a-dual-career -marriage.

Walters, N. 2016. "Here's What a Former Apple CEO Wishes He Could Have Told Himself When He Took Over the Tech Giant at Age 44." *Business Insider,* March 4. http:// www.businessinsider.com/what-john-sculley-wishes-he-knew-when-he-became -apple-ceo-2016-3.

Walton, B. 2016. Interview by KTVK-TV. April 26. https://www.youtube.com/watch?v =XhQG2dP2AHc.

Wang, L., and J. K. Murnighan. 2013. "The Generalist Bias." *Organizational Behavior and Human Decision Processes* 120 (1): 47–61.

Warner, A. 2017. "What Didn't Kill Colin Hodge Made Him Stronger." *Mixergy* (podcast), June 30. https://mixergy.com/interviews/what-didnt-kill-colin-hodge-made -him-stronger.

Wasserman, N. 2002. "The Venture Capitalist as Entrepreneur: Characteristics and Dynamics Within VC Firms." PhD diss., Harvard University, Boston, MA.

———. 2004. "Ockham Technologies: Living on the Razor's Edge." Harvard Business School Case 804-129. https://www.hbs.edu/faculty/pages/item.aspx?num=30839.

———. 2008. "The Founder's Dilemma." *Harvard Business Review* 86 (2): 102–109.

———. 2012. *The Founder's Dilemmas: Anticipating and Avoiding the Pitfalls That Can Sink a Startup.* Princeton, NJ: Princeton University Press.

———. 2017. "The Throne vs. the Kingdom: Founder Control and Value Creation in Startups." *Strategic Management Journal* 38:255–277.

Wasserman, N., and Y. Braid. 2012. "Family Matters at ProLab." Harvard Business School Case 813-130. https://www.hbs.edu/faculty/Pages/item.aspx?num=43829.

Wasserman, N., J. J., Bussgang, and R. Gordon. 2010. "Curt Schilling's Next Pitch." Harvard Business School Case 810-053. https://www.hbs.edu/faculty/Pages/item.aspx?num=38236.

Wasserman, N., and R. Galper. 2008. "Big to Small: The Two Lives of Barry Nalls." Harvard Business School Case 808-167. https://www.hbs.edu/faculty/Pages/item.aspx?num=36102.

Wasserman, N., and M. Marx. 2008. "Split Decisions: How Social and Economic Choices Affect the Stability of Founding Teams." Paper presented at Academy of Management Annual Meeting, Anaheim, CA, August.

Wasserman, N., and L. P. Maurice. 2008a. "Savage Beast (A)." Harvard Business School Case 809-069. https://www.hbs.edu/faculty/Pages/item.aspx?num=36725.

———. 2008b. "Savage Beast (B)." Harvard Business School Supplement 809-096. https://www.hbs.edu/faculty/Pages/item.aspx?num=36726.

Wiener-Bronner, D., and C. Alesci, C. 2017. "Chobani CEO Finds Trump's Travel Ban 'Personal for Me.'" *CNN Money*, January 30. http://money.cnn.com/2017/01/30/news/chobani-response-travel-ban.

Wilkinson, A. 2015. "What Elon Musk and Reid Hoffman Learned from Failing Wisely." *Inc.*, February 23. http://www.inc.com/amy-wilkinson/why-the-best-leaders-fail-wisely.html.

Wilson, T. D., and D. T. Gilbert. 2003. "Affective Forecasting." *Advances in Experimental Social Psychology* 35:345–411.

Wolfinger, N. 2015. "Want to Avoid Divorce? Wait to Get Married, but Not Too Long." Institute for Family Studies, July 16. https://ifstudies.org/blog/want-to-avoid-divorce-wait-to-get-married-but-not-too-long.

Wozniak, S., with G. Smith. 2006. *iWoz: Computer Geek to Cult Icon.* New York: Norton.

Wu, Y., H. A. Schwartz, D. Stillwell, and M. Kosinski. 2017. "Birds of a Feather Do Flock Together: Behavior-Based Personality-Assessment Method Reveals Personality Similarity Among Couples and Friends." *Psychological Science* 28 (3): 276–284.

Wuchty, S., B. F. Jones, and B. Uzzi. 2007. "The Increasing Dominance of Teams in Production of Knowledge." *Science* 316 (5827): 1036–1039.

Zimmerman, E. 2015. "Start-Up Blends Old-Fashioned Matchmaking and Algorithms." *New York Times*, April 22. https://www.nytimes.com/2015/04/23/business/smallbusiness/start-up-blends-old-fashioned-matchmaking-and-algorithms.html.

INDEX

Italic page numbers indicate material in figures.